Abraham's

Faith

A 30-Day Women's Devotional Based on the
Life of Abraham

M a r y   J a n e   H u m e s

All Scripture quotations, unless otherwise indicated, are from the Authorized (King James) Version. Rights in the Authorized Version in the United Kingdom are vested in the Crown. Reproduced by permission of the Crown's patentee, Cambridge University Press.

Proofreading and typesetting: Sally Hanan of Inksnatcher.com
Cover design: GetCovers

Ordering Information: Quantity sales. Special discounts are available on quantity purchases by corporations, associations, and others. For details, contact the author at hello@maryjanehumes.com.

Abraham's Faith: A 30-Day Women's Devotional Based on the Life of Abraham/Mary Jane Humes

ISBN Print: 978-1-7360389-8-7

ISBN E-Book: 978-1-7360389-7-0

This book is lovingly dedicated to my maternal grandfather, Clarence Lester Hornberger (July 13, 1903– February 4, 2003). He was truly a good and godly man whose daily prayer was for precious souls to be saved.

.

Contents

Introduction

Abraham's Faith

This is the biblical story and journey of Abraham and of his faith in God. Abraham's great faith in Him, I believe, rests in the fact that Abraham had such a close friendship with God. Abraham was the only person specifically called "the friend of God." This personal friendship with God has much to teach us, even as we, too, strive to have a close relationship with Him.

In each chapter, the section "Thoughts from Mother Sarah" is derived from the verse in 1 Peter 3:6, "Even as Sara obeyed Abraham, calling him lord: *whose daughters ye are*, as long as ye do well, and are not afraid with any amazement" (emphasis added). This is my attempt, as an author, to speak for Sarah (in her voice, giving her advice, and speaking as a woman with great personal desires). She was the wife of a great man, and today speaks to us as a joyful mother reaching down across the centuries to all of her spiritual daughters. It is my heart's desire that she would be pleased and honored by the words I have attributed to her.

It is also my desire that this devotional will draw you closer to Christ, help you in your Christian walk, and give you a glimpse of the depth and richness of God's Word.

Thank you for reading.

In Christ,

Mary Jane Humes

Author's Note

Many times in Scripture, and sometimes in my writing, the word "Lord" is used when referring to a particular passage of Scripture. This designation with all capital letters is not a typo, nor is it used to show importance. Many times the name of God, referred to as Lord, is the translation of *Jehovah* in the Old Testament.

The reason for all capitals versus the capital "L" followed by lowercase letters is to differentiate the meanings between two different Hebrew words, both translated into the English language as "Lord." The word translated into the English language from the Hebrew is Lord, all capitals, denoting God's personal name. The word "Lord" (as compared to Lord) is one of His titles. Psalm 8:1 "O Lord our Lord…" is an excellent example, showing the reader there are different meanings for the same word. The word "Lord" (Jehovah) is not a title of God; it is rather a name of God, specifically God's personal name.

When the Bible uses the name Lord, the writer is implying a closeness, a friendship, between God and the speaker. It is saying the mighty Creator God and the speaker are on a first-name basis. It is similar to calling your friend by her first name rather than the more formal but very accurate title of Mrs. Jones, for example. When you see the name of God as Lord—all capital letters, know God is showing us that He and the one using His name have a close, friendly, trusting relationship. Many Bible scholars, and I, too, believe the names of both Jehovah and Lord refer to the second Person of the Godhead, none other than the preincarnate Jesus Christ.

Day 1

Abram's Early Years

BIBLE READING: GENESIS 11:27–32

LEARNING ABOUT FATHER ABRAHAM: About three hundred years after the great flood of Noah, and nine generations later, one descendant of Noah's son Shem was a man named Terah. The Bible records that Shem lived for five hundred years after the flood, so Terah and his sons, Nahor, Haran, and Abram were contemporaries of Shem. Terah lived with his family in the city of Ur of the Chaldees. In this city, Terah's son Haran died and left behind a son, Lot. Terah's two other sons got married: Nahor to a woman named Milcah and Abram to Sarai. Abram's name meant "high father," but despite this epithet, he and Sarai could not have any children because it appeared Sarai was barren.

According to Bible scholars, the city of Ur was a rich and modern city for its time. It was filled with idol worshippers, and its major god was the moon god, Nanna. There is not much known about Abram's life in this city, but Abram knew his history: the account of creation, the fall of the first parents, the method of sacrificing innocent animals, knowing which animals were considered "clean," the murder of Abel by his brother, the flood of Noah, the worship of God by Noah and Shem after the flood, and the confusion of languages at the Tower of Babel. Abram also knew the mysterious promise that the LORD God gave the first parents—the promised seed of the woman that was to come would first be bruised by the serpent but would then triumphantly crush the serpent's head. The first parents enjoyed a friendship with their creator, but, in Abram's time, it seemed few people were interested in such a friendship.

There must have been a longing in the heart of Abram to commune with the LORD God, like Adam had when God walked and talked with him. Abram knew God wanted a relationship with His creation, and he wanted an audience with the creator Himself. Unlike others around him, Abram realized it was wrong to worship other gods such as the moon god the people of Ur worshiped. Abram reached out to worship God following the pattern that God had taught Adam and Noah. His desire and worship did not go unrewarded. One day, God appeared to Abram and gave him specific directions—he was to leave his country and family and go to an unknown land.

When Abram received this call from God, he most likely told his father, Terah, what he intended to do, Terah thought Abram had a good idea and did not want to be left out, so

2

Terah and his orphaned grandson, Lot, accompanied Abram and Sarai when they left Ur of Chaldees to go to this unknown land. However, before they got to their destination, they stopped and settled in Haran for several years until Terah passed away at the age of 205.

THOUGHTS FROM MOTHER SARAH

Early in my relationship with my husband, I called him "lord." I remembered what our creator told our first mother, Eve—that her husband would rule over her. I loved Abram and I love our creator, so I wanted to please them both while simultaneously harnessing my quarrelsome, contentious, and bossy sprit, which is what my name "Sarai" means.

Abram said that when I called him Lord, I looked so beautiful! He made it easy for me to refer to him as Lord because he was my leader, my guardian, my lover, my counselor, and my cheerleader. He encouraged me to do the things that brought me personal joy and satisfaction.

My daughters, it is not a sign of weakness when you choose to obey your husband. Submitting yourself to your husband frees you to be the complete, fulfilled, and vibrant woman that you desire to be.

BECOMING A FRIEND OF GOD

If we want a friendship with God, and His blessings too, Abram shows us the way. Although not recorded, Abram must have sought, learned, and researched all he could about the creator God to better worship Him.

Every relationship has its own set of protocols, and becoming a friend of God is no different. If we want to be a friend of God, worship Him, please Him, and have a relationship with Him, then we must also do things His way. Although we come to God just as we are, God loves us enough to not allow us to stay that way.

With any friendship we pursue, we need to find out how we can seek to please our new friend. Having a friendship with God is no different. We learn what God desires and then do the things that are pleasing to Him.

Like Abram, when we seek to be a friend of God, we may find ourselves in the minority. While there are many who give lip service to God and say they belong to God—and they just might—those who seek a solid friendship with God will sometimes find themselves at odds with others who do not seek the same kind of relationship with Him. But God knows the intentions and the hearts of all men and those who seek Him and desire to be His friends are incredibly special to Him. These are the people God calls closer to Him to receive His special blessings.

Words from Abraham's God

Genesis 3:15 I will put enmity between thee and the woman, and between thy seed and her seed; it shall bruise thy head, and thou shalt bruise his heel.

John 15:15 Henceforth I call you not servants; for the servant knoweth not what his lord doeth: but I have called you friends;

for all things that I have heard of my Father I have made known unto you.

Acts 7:2–3 He [Peter] said, Men, brethren, and fathers, hearken; The God of glory appeared unto our father Abraham, when he was in Mesopotamia, before he dwelt in Charran, And said unto him, Get thee out of thy country, and from thy kindred, and come into the land which I shall shew thee.

James 2:23 The scripture was fulfilled which saith, Abraham believed God, and it was imputed unto him for righteousness: and he was called the Friend of God.

1 Peter 3:4–6 Let it be the hidden man of the heart, in that which is not corruptible, even the ornament of a meek and quiet spirit, which is in the sight of God of great price. For after this manner in the old time the holy women also, who trusted in God, adorned themselves, being in subjection unto their own husbands: Even as Sara obeyed Abraham, calling him lord: whose daughters ye are, as long as ye do well, and are not afraid with any amazement.

Prayer

Dear heavenly Father, help me see the benefits of choosing You as my very best friend. Without You, I can do nothing. You have been so good to me, and You loved me before I knew You. So now help me, despite my frail, sinful, human condition, to love You in return. Help me do, daily, what honors and pleases You. Draw me closer to You that others may see my desire to be Your friend and see that You are my friend as well. I ask this in Your perfect Son's name, amen.

DAY 2

God's Promises in Canaan

BIBLE READING — GENESIS 12:1–7

LEARNING ABOUT FATHER ABRAHAM: Abraham's father, Terah, died after Abram and Sarai had been living in Haran for several years. After his death, Abram remembered the LORD's initial command and knew it was not God's plan for him to stay in Haran. The land that God promised to Abram was still unknown to him. God promised Abram that He would:

1. Make Abram a great nation.
2. Bless Abram.
3. Make Abram's name great.
4. Bless all the families of the earth through Abram.
5. Give the land of Canaan to Abram's descendants.

If these fantastic promises were not enough, God also told Abram that He would bless those who blessed Abram and curse those who cursed him.

7

Abram, at seventy-five years old, left Haran with his wife Sarai, his nephew Lot, and their servants and journeyed to the unfamiliar land of promise called Canaan. Once they arrived there, the LORD again appeared to Abram and told him that the land currently filled with Canaanites would someday belong to Abram's descendants. Abram responded to these great promises of God by worshipping Him. There he built a permanent altar in this unknown land so he could have communion with God—his friend—and he offered a sacrifice to Him there.

Abram, the newcomer, had unusual practices that differed from the culture of the native Canaanite people. They watched this foreigner as he worshipped his God.

The promises of God to Abram were unconditional. God said that He would fulfill them regardless of what Abram would or would not do. God fulfilled some of these promises in Abram's lifetime, but most of them reached far beyond his death and continue even to our present day.

1. Abram became the progenitor of the Jewish and Arab races.

2. Abram was a rich man.

3. Proponents of the three major monotheistic world religions—Judaism, Christianity, and Islam—all revere the name of Abram.

4. Jesus Christ came through the line of Abram, and through Him, all the earth was and is blessed.

8

Thoughts from Mother Sarah

When my lord moved us into the land God told him we were to go to, I sometimes felt lonely and even afraid in this unfamiliar place that my lord called the land of promise. While the promise God gave to my lord was great, the one thing I focused on was having a child. I was sixty-five years old; and although some women lived to be well over one hundred years old and had babies, even in their seventies, I knew I was closer to the end rather than the beginning of my childbearing years.

When we talked about my becoming a mother, Abram wondered if perhaps our child would be the seed of the woman that our creator God had promised to our first parents Adam and Eve.

Becoming a Friend of God

After Abram received his great promises from God, he responded by worshipping God, and his worship included a sacrifice. The Bible mentions "the sacrifice of praise" and "the sacrifice of thanksgiving." A sacrifice implies that something needs to be killed.

Giving God our thanks is a sacrifice of sorts: when we are thanking God for His blessings, we are refraining from asking something of Him. The sacrifices of praise and thanksgiving get our mind and our focus away from us—"killing" that focus—and instead redirect our focus to God, the source of all the good things we enjoy every day.

Just as the promises God gave Abram were unconditional, so, too, does God offer us unconditional promises. When we accept His wonderful gift of salvation, He has promised to take our soul to heaven, despite what we choose to do or not do in this life. He keeps our soul, and there is nothing we can do that will nullify this great promise of His. If you have received His wonderful gift of eternal life, take some time to thank Him for the safety of your eternal soul.

While God is the ultimate source of our blessings, God uses people to help and provide for us. These people should have our sincere thanks as well. Make it a point to say thank you often. When was the last time you thanked your boss or your husband for something nice they did? Or your children for the joy they bring to you? Or your pastor for his preaching and his prayers? Or your friends for their friendship?

Being thankful to God for all His blessings and showing our thanks to others—for allowing God to use them to bless our lives—makes us stand out among so many other people. It is both a refreshing and unusual attitude in our world today. Just as the native Canaanites watched Abram make his altar and give thanks to his God, so, too, are we being watched by those who do not put their faith in Christ. A Christian who is truly thankful for all of God's blessings is a testimony to others.

Words from Abraham's God

John 3:16 God so loved the world, that he gave his only begotten Son, that whosoever believeth in him should not perish, but have everlasting life.

2 Timothy 3:2 Men shall be lovers of their own selves, covetous, boasters, proud, blasphemers, disobedient to parents, unthankful, unholy.

Hebrews 11:8 By faith Abraham, when he was called to go out into a place which he should after receive for an inheritance, obeyed; and he went out, not knowing whither he went.

Hebrews 13:15 By him therefore let us offer the sacrifice of praise to God continually, that is, the fruit of our lips giving thanks to his name.

James 1:17 Every good gift and every perfect gift is from above, and cometh down from the Father of lights, with whom is no variableness, neither shadow of turning.

Prayer

Dear heavenly Father, thank You for creating me. Thank You for desiring my company so much that You went to great lengths to secure my soul to be with You forever. You have blessed me so greatly in this life as well. Thank You for a body and a mind that works. Thank You for my electricity and indoor plumbing; for a closet with changes of clothing and several pairs of shoes; for my shampoo, toothpaste, and pretty jewelry that You delighted to give me. These are just a few of my many, everyday blessings.

Thank You for all the food that I can enjoy. Thank You for the blessings of my family and friends. Thank You for Your love, which does not end when I die but ushers me into even greater and better blessings. Thank You for Your great and unspeakable gift of salvation to me. Amen.

DAY 3

Into Egypt

BIBLE READING — GENESIS 12:10–20

LEARNING ABOUT FATHER ABRAHAM: Living in the promised land of Canaan had its trials. Although God had given wonderful promises to Abram concerning his personal future and his future descendants, Abram and his household encountered the problem of famine. This food shortage was serious and troubling. In search of necessary food, Abram took things into his own hands. Instead of waiting for further instructions from the Lord, he took his household with him and fled toward Egypt.

Close to the border of Egypt, Abram again failed to trust the LORD to keep both him and Sarai safe, and he requested that Sarai masquerade as his sister rather than be known as his wife. Even at sixty-five years old, Sarai was a beautiful woman, and Abram feared that one or more of the Egyptian men would desire Sarai so much that they would kill him to have her.

After Abram and Sarai entered Egypt, the attractive Sarai caused a stir among the Egyptian men. They recommended this seemingly single and eligible foreigner to Pharaoh, perhaps as a potential addition to his harem, and they took Sarai into Pharaoh's house. As a reward for Sarai, Pharaoh gave Abram, whom Pharaoh believed was Sarai's brother, many gifts of both livestock and servants. Meanwhile, while Sarai was a guest of Pharaoh, the LORD had His hand of protection upon her and sent plagues upon Pharaoh and his household because of Pharaoh's unholy intentions toward the married Sarai.

Somehow, Pharaoh connected the plagues with the lovely foreign woman and realized that he was courting a married and thus unavailable woman. Realizing his honest mistake, Pharaoh sternly rebuked Abram for his deception, admitting that he had considered making Sarai one of his wives. Pharaoh was justifiably angry with Abram, and even with Sarai, and had his men eject them from Egypt.

THOUGHTS FROM MOTHER SARAH

This journey into Egypt was a horrible time in my life. I didn't want to go to Egypt, but food became so scarce in Canaan. Then my lord Abram asked me to say that I was not his wife but his sister—a single woman! I knew Abram wanted to protect me; nevertheless, I didn't like the deception. In this time of uncertainty, I wanted even more protection from my husband, not less. But I followed the leading of my lord and trusted that he knew what was best for me and the others who came with us.

Then they took me into Pharaoh's house. I was lonely, scared, and, yes, angry at Abram for leaving Canaan and lying about our marriage. Abram was alive, well, and free, and since Pharaoh thought I was a single woman, he wanted to take me for his wife. My husband made a huge mistake because he did not trust God to take care of us in Canaan.

My dear daughters, I hope that you have a husband you can trust to always do right by you. But sometimes, despite his best intentions, your husband may unintentionally hurt you. After all, he is only human. It is only God who you can completely rely upon to help both you and your husband.

BECOMING A FRIEND OF GOD

Just because we are in the place where God wants us, just because we are doing His will, does not mean that we will not be immune to problems. A preacher once said, "When you are right with God, don't expect a new car, rather, expect your old car to blow up." While this may be extreme, when we are living in the will of God and serving Him, God sometimes allows trials and temptations to come to test our faith and ultimately strengthen us. Problems and challenges are a part of this life, regardless of serving God. Since you know you will have difficulties in this life, it is a wise thing to determine to inquire of God in all your decisions, especially when troubles arise.

Taking action to overcome our challenges is a good thing. But even while we move forward to help ourselves, we need to ask God for His direction and trust Him to take care of us. We will have times when we make wrong choices, when we think only of our ourselves and believe we have the "perfect solutions" to our problems. The beautiful thing is that God, who gives us free will, who allows us to make our own choices, still watches over us and will deliver us, just like He did for Abram and

Sarai. Sometimes parents will allow their child to do something they know will not work out the way the child wants; but the parent, like our heavenly Father, oversees the child's efforts and lends a helping hand at the first cry of distress.

When difficulties arise, first ask God for His direction and His leading. Our problems do not surprise Him. If God has blessed you with a husband, God leads you through your husband. Our husbands have the final say. When we submit to our husbands, even when our husbands are wrong (and we all know that sometimes they are!), God does, and will, work things out for our good. When we submit to our husbands, we are submitting to God Himself, who commanded us to submit in the first place. So then, the next time your husband wants to do something you have doubts about, express your opinions to him but allow your husband to make the final decision. Keep in mind that it is no longer your husband you are submitting to, it is God Himself. God can and will take care of you even better than your husband.

Words from Abraham's God

Proverbs 3:5 Trust in the LORD with all thine heart; and lean not unto thine own understanding.

1 Chronicles 16:21 He suffered no man to do them wrong: yea, he reproved kings for their sakes.

Ephesians 5:25 Husbands, love your wives, even as Christ also loved the church, and gave himself for it.

Philippians 2:4 Look not every man on his own things, but every man also on the things of others.

Hebrews 13:6 We may boldly say, The Lord is my helper, and I will not fear what man shall do unto me.

Prayer

Dear heavenly Father, when I face problems, help me to trust in You, to focus on You, and to continue the work You have given me to do. When I'm looking for solutions and trying to solve situations, as You expect me to do, let me focus on and trust You more so that You will receive the honor, glory, and praise.

Please guide and help my husband to be wise and to make the right decisions for our family, but help me put my ultimate trust in You rather than in him. Thank You for Your mercies, Your kindness, Your love, and Your daily care for me, which truly is new every morning. Thank You that when I fail, You don't give up on me. But help me fail You less and trust You more. I ask this in the name of Christ, amen.

Separation of Abram and Lot

BIBLE READING — GENESIS 13: 1–13

LEARNING ABOUT FATHER ABRAHAM: After being commanded to leave Egypt, Abram, Sarai, and all who were with them returned to the southern part of Canaan. The Bible mentions "the south" twice in these verses, but it is referring to two distinct southern places.

Abram returned to the southern part of Canaan from the land of Egypt, his ultimate goal being to get back to where he had started some time before: Bethel—the house of God. Abram did not have a house in the land of Canaan. His "house" was a movable, temporary dwelling—a tent. He could have settled anywhere, but Abram wanted to return to the altar he had built at Bethel prior to the famine that forced him to go to Egypt.

After returning to Bethel, a new family problem arose. Abram and his nephew Lot had so many cattle and servants that there was not enough room in the land for the herds of both men.

Tension built between the two groups while they constantly maneuvered for the best grazing land, while also respecting each other's boundaries. It would not be long before the discord would involve the two masters, Abram and Lot.

Wisely, Abram knew he had to keep peace and good relations between himself and his nephew, so he told Lot that it was time to separate. Generously, Abram gave Lot the first choice of land. As Lot considered his options, he looked over the plain of Jordan and saw its lush, fertile acres of prime grazing land. Perhaps Uncle Abram remarked to his nephew that the plain of Jordan reminded him of what he imagined the garden of Eden was like long ago. Lot saw that this land in the east was the more desirable option and moved there. He pitched his tent in the plain of Jordan in an area that overlooked the city of Sodom. The Bible points out that the men of Sodom "were wicked and sinners before the LORD exceedingly" (Genesis 13:13).

Meanwhile, Abram stayed near Bethel. This was the first time since Abram had left Ur of the Chaldees that he had completely separated himself from all of his other family members.

THOUGHTS FROM MOTHER SARAH

I was glad to get back to Bethel. The land of Canaan, which at first seemed so foreign to me, was now my home. I was enjoying the services of my new Egyptian maid, Hagar. She was respectful, hardworking, and attentive to my every wish. But when my lord told me about the conflicts between our herdsman and Lot's, I knew it was time for Lot and his family to finally leave our community.

Lot was almost like a son to Abram and me, but although he was a good man, I didn't see in our nephew the love and desire to worship our creator like my lord had. Lot was a grown man, and he, with his wife, children, and servants, needed space to live his life the way he saw fit. I knew I would miss having Lot's family nearby, but I hoped that his absence would soon be filled with our own promised child.

BECOMING A FRIEND OF GOD

This passage teaches us about the principle of separation. If you are the total of your five closest friends, then choose your friends carefully. Sometimes friends, and even family members, become troublesome and can threaten your personal peace. Loving yourself enough to separate from those who negatively affect you, or from those who live in open sin (I Corinthians 5:9–11), is not a bad thing. Rather, it is a vital element of self-care to protect yourself and your Christian walk.

When you refuse to separate yourself from those who are openly living in sin, you are condoning their sinful lifestyle and becoming an accomplice in their sin. When a person desires to continue in his or her sinful ways, that is their personal decision. But you, too, have a decision to make, and that is to distance yourself from them.

This does not mean that you stop loving them, stop praying for them, or hate them. Separation is loving your Savior, and yourself, so much that you only want what is best in your life so that you can offer your purest service to Christ. Realize that whoever you allow close to you must also share the desire that God's will for you is more important than any human relationship.

Separating from people can also prevent a strained relationship from getting worse. It is difficult, especially when you find yourself needing distance from a family member, such as a wayward, grown child or an overbearing, controlling parent. The end goal of separation is not isolation but a wake-up call to the offending party, with the desire that they will mend their ways and seek reconciliation with both you and God. When a relationship becomes toxic, or when a person close to you is openly living in unrepentant sin, it is vital for you to separate from them.

Words from Abraham's God

Proverbs 13:20 He that walketh with wise men shall be wise: but a companion of fools shall be destroyed.

Romans 16:17 I beseech you, brethren, mark them which cause divisions and offences contrary to the doctrine which ye have learned; and avoid them.

Romans 12:18 If it be possible, as much as lieth in you, live peaceably with all men.

1 Corinthians 5:11 I have written unto you not to keep company, if any man that is called a brother be a fornicator, or covetous, or an idolater, or a railer, or a drunkard, or an extortioner; with such an one no not to eat.

2 Thessalonians 3:6 Now we command you, brethren, in the name of our Lord Jesus Christ, that ye withdraw yourselves from every brother that walketh disorderly, and not after the tradition which he received of us.

Prayer

Dear heavenly Father, thank You for the friends and the family You have blessed me with. I love them all so much, but help me to be both wise and strong in my relationships.

When those who are close to me are openly sinning—when they have anger or control issues, when our meetings are tense and filled with stress and I am happier to see them leave rather than come—then help me to love myself and to love You enough to separate me from their company, so that I would neither condone their behavior nor be like them. Help me to do so humbly, knowing that except for Your great grace, I would be just like them or worse. I ask this in the name of Your perfect Son, Christ Jesus, amen.

DAY 5

The Dust of the Earth

BIBLE READING — GENESIS 13:14–18

LEARNING ABOUT FATHER ABRAHAM: After Abram and his nephew amicably parted company, the LORD appeared to Abram again with a special, wonderful, and important message that was meant just for him. God instructed Abram to look in all four of the cardinal directions—all the land God had promised to the still childless man—and declared that He would give it to his seed forever. God promised Abram that his "seed," his children, would be as many "as the dust of the earth."

Abram might have picked up a handful of dirt from the ground and remembered that his God, the creator, made the first man, Adam, from the dust of the earth. Abram knew Adam was a physical being and that he was made of dust too. Abram also realized that the reference to dust meant that this promise from God was that Abram would have innumerable, live, physical descendants! Abram's offspring, his children, would constantly multiply and fill this God-given land.

Then God told Abram that he was to take a walk in the land of his inheritance. So Abram packed up his tent and journeyed. While traveling, he perhaps not only admired the scenery but also felt the rough rocks and soft grass, listened to the wind whistling and the birds chirping, smelled the fresh air, and ate of the sweet fruit that this land produced. Abram and Sarai both might have imagined people living there—not just any people but their very own children, grandchildren, and great-grandchildren. In their wonderment, they most likely thanked and praised God.

Abram finally pitched his tent and settled his household on the plain of Mamre, not very far from the city of Sodom. And as was Abram's faithful practice after moving to a new location, he built a place of worship, an altar, where he could meet with and commune with his friend, God. Abram's altar was a physical place for a physical man to connect with a spiritual God.

THOUGHTS FROM MOTHER SARAH

When my lord told me about the latest message from the LORD, it was the encouragement I needed. This message gave me hope that I would have a child. I was wondering if my lord had misunderstood or whether God had something else in mind for us. But it seemed that God was still going to give me the desire of my heart—a baby t I would give birth to, hold, cuddle, nurse, and watch grow. It made me smile every time I thought about having a baby of my very own.

My dear daughters, I know from experience that it is hard to wait on God. We want more than to simply hear His promises; we also want to receive immediately what He has promised to us. Yet I have learned that God's timing is not our timing and that there are still blessings for us, even as we wait on Him.

BECOMING A FRIEND OF GOD

Sometimes there has to be loss before there is gain. Abram lost the companionship of relatives when he separated from Lot and his family, but shortly afterward, Abram received the message from God that he would gain innumerable physical descendants who would fill the land. While the loss of Lot was immediate and the promise of children was still in the future, Abram filled this time gap with the worship of his God. While Abram did not have the physical blessings of offspring at that point in his life, he had the spiritual blessing of communion with his God. In this world, we may not get to enjoy physical blessings when we desire them, but when we might lack in physical blessings, we can take some time to seek and enjoy spiritual ones.

Many times our focus is primarily on the physical and we neglect the spiritual aspect of our lives. Lack of physical blessings is not a sign that our God has deserted us, rather, it can be a sign that we need to draw closer to our God. Since we are both physical and spiritual beings, we also have spiritual needs. When we don't make the time to meet our spiritual needs, we can sometimes suffer in physical ways. Learning and appreciating God in the physical realm is preparation for loving Him and knowing Him spiritually.

While Abram looked forward to his physical offspring and enjoyed the blessing of his physical land, he did not neglect to pay attention to his spiritual needs, which resulted in communion with his God. Many, if not all things, in this physical realm, such as Abram's altar and our Bible, are not just material objects but are also portals into the spiritual realm.

Words from Abraham's God

Psalm 68:19 Blessed be the Lord, who daily loadeth us with benefits, even the God of our salvation. Selah.

Ecclesiastes 2:24 There is nothing better for a man, than that he should eat and drink, and that he should make his soul enjoy good in his labor. This also I saw it was from the hand of God.

Matthew 6:31–32 Take no thought, saying, What shall we eat? or, What shall we drink? or, Wherewithal shall we be clothed? (For after all these things do the Gentiles seek:) for your heavenly Father knoweth that ye have need of all these things.

John 1:2 Beloved, I wish above all things that thou mayest prosper and be in health, even as thy soul prospereth.

Acts 7:5 He gave him none inheritance in it, no, not so much as to set his foot on: yet he promised he would give it to him for a possession, and to his seed after him, when as yet he had no child.

Prayer

Dear heavenly Father, thank You for all the good You have given me. You deserve all my worship and my praise. You deserve far more than I can ever give You, but help me to offer You my feeble attempts to worship and praise You daily. In troublesome times of separation, let me see Your great goodness through the eyes of faith. Thank You so much for Your never-failing love for me and for all that You have promised me yet to come. In Jesus's name I ask this, amen.

Abram Delivers Lot

BIBLE READING — GENESIS 14:1–16

LEARNING ABOUT FATHER ABRAHAM: Abram, Sarai, and their servants were in the land of Canaan where there was political unrest and rumors of war, and this instability affected them. Genesis 14:1–11 gives us a snapshot of that time and of the people who lived there. This passage of Scripture also records the first war mentioned in the Bible. Abram, the peacemaker from chapter 13, showed that although he was peaceful, he was not passive. God promised to protect Abram, but part of that protection was giving Abram the foresight to employ and train his servants in the art of war. In this chapter, Abram became a man of the sword, a general with an army to command.

After twelve years of forced tribute (taxation), five oriental kings rebelled and went to war against their oppressor and chieftain, King Chedorlaomer, and three other confederate kings. This war took place in the Valley of Siddim (the Bible calls this a vale), which was full of slime pits. This slippery valley was a treacherous place to wage a war; the slime pits claimed the lives of many foot soldiers, including the reigning king of Sodom. With the four kings of Canaan dispatched, the oriental soldiers looted the city of Sodom and took food, treasures, and human captives, and among them was Lot, Abram's nephew.

Out of all the captives, one unidentified person escaped. He ran to "Abram the Hebrew" for help. Lot, who knew his uncle was the single person who could, and hopefully would, help all of them, might have directed the escapee to Abram. When Abram got the message that they had taken Lot captive, he had compassion on Lot and was immediately moved to help. Abram took 318 of his trained servants and, aided by his military confederates Mamre, Eshcol, and Aner and their men, went to rescue Lot and the others.

Abram's aim was twofold: he wanted to free the captives and defeat the enemy. Using some brilliant military strategy, Abram and his army pursued the enemy to where the victors and their captives camped in an area called Dan, which is in the Jordan River valley. Once he caught up with them, Abram divided his army and, under the cover of night, attacked Chedorlaomer, freed the captives, recovered all the war booty, and chased the invaders north for about one hundred miles to Hobah, near the border of Syria. He wanted to make sure they would leave his land. This is the only biblically recorded military action Abram took part in, and his only motive was to help free his nephew.

Had Lot not associated with the wicked men of Sodom, he would not have been among the captives who endured the accompanying fear and humiliation. Ironically, it might have been Lot who ensured the rescue of all the other captives by requesting Abram the Hebrew's help. This is the first place in Scripture where Abram is identified as a Hebrew. According to Bible scholars, the word "Hebrew" means "one that has crossed over." This presumably refers to the Euphrates River, which Abram crossed when he left Ur of the Chaldees. The term "Hebrew" also connotes the idea of a nomad rather than a settled resident of the land.

THOUGHTS FROM MOTHER SARAH

My lord Abram taught us that part of our safety was in preparing a powerful defense. We knew our God would take care of us, but my lord knew God also expected him to do his part. It was wise of my lord to strengthen, train, and arm our servants in case of any attack. My dear daughters, let the example of my lord be a pattern for you too. Your battles may not be physical, but I encourage you to pray daily for God's protection for all that He has given you. Your prayers for safety are a spiritual defense against the attacks of the enemy.

BECOMING A FRIEND OF GOD

While there is a time for peace, there is also a time and need for war. This passage of Scripture teaches us that when a brother or sister needs help and has asked for it, it is our responsibility to act on their behalf.

Some things may be too much for us to handle by ourselves, and we might need some help also. Abram had allies, and he was not too proud to ask them to unite with him in this dangerous endeavor. Abram had a good testimony among his neighbors, so much so that they were willing to join him when he got Lot's message. We, too, need to have a reputation among others that is honorable. The New Testament describes this as having "a good report of them which are without" (1 Timothy 3:7).

There is everything right in having a good working relationship with unbelievers in this world. While we Christian women need to separate ourselves from the sinful actions of the world, we cannot become isolationists. Those of the world may not understand or accept our Christian faith but striving to establish and maintain a good rapport with them is an opportunity to be a testimony while we benefit from their knowledge and friendship.

God has placed unbelievers in our lives for a purpose, both for their benefit and ours. Endeavor to have a good rapport with unbelievers while you represent your Savior and maintain your personal Christian testimony.

Words from Abraham's God

Proverbs 17:17 A friend loveth at all times, and a brother is born for adversity.

Ecclesiastes 3:8 A time to love, and a time to hate; a time of war, and a time of peace.

Isaiah 41:2 & 3 Who raised up the righteous man from the east, called him to his foot, gave the nations before him, and made him rule over kings? he gave them as the dust to his sword, and as driven stubble to his bow. He pursued them, and passed safely; even by the way that he had not gone with his feet.

Galatians 6:2 Bear ye one another's burdens, and so fulfill the law of Christ.

2 Corinthians 10:4 The weapons of our warfare are not carnal, but mighty through God to the pulling down of strong holds.

Prayer

Dear heavenly Father, thank You for the people You have brought into my life. Let me always be a blessing to both believers and nonbelievers alike, whether they are family members, employers, coworkers, or my friends.

Please give me discernment and direction when I am asked to help others so that I may do so out of pure motives, and give me wisdom to know what to do or say, or not do or say. Help me use the spiritual weapon of prayer to fight my battles, whether the conflicts are for me or to help others.

Help me pray more, not less, for my country, my church, and my family; and for Your protection upon us. In all that I do, I ask that You ultimately receive the glory, honor, and praise of my actions and decisions. In Jesus's name, amen.

Melchizedek and the King of Sodom

BIBLE READING — GENESIS 14:17–24

LEARNING ABOUT FATHER ABRAHAM: After the battle in which he defeated and freed the captives, including Lot, and roundly ousted the troublemakers, Abram became an immediate and well-deserving war hero. Two kings congratulated Abram on his victory. The first was Melchizedek, the king of Salem (Salem means "peace"), who was also a priest of God. Melchizedek came to give a spiritual blessing and to celebrate Abram's victory with the physical blessing of food. This mysterious, historical figure, who was both a king and a priest, is a subject of much study and debate. Whoever he truly was, Abram recognized him as a messenger from God and as one who was grateful for God's help in his victory. Abram generously gave Melchizedek "tithes of all," or about ten percent of the spoils of war.

Immediately after Abram's meeting with Melchizedek, another king, the king of Sodom, approached Abram. He was possibly a son of the original king of Sodom who had perished in the slime pits (Genesis 14:10). Unlike Melchizedek, who came to give something to Abram, the king of Sodom wanted something from Abram—the people Abram had freed. Knowing that the allegiance of these former captives was by default to Abram their deliverer, the king of Sodom offered Abram all the recovered goods in exchange for the former captives.

Abram refused the spoils of war from the king of Sodom. He went to war only with the intention of freeing Lot and the others. Freeing the other captives and gaining the spoils of war were just extras. Although he was glad for both, Abram would not take advantage of the situation.

As the victor in the war, Abram had the power to take the people, make them his servants, and keep all their belongings for himself. But Abram told this heathen king that he had promised the most high God that he would neither accept the goods nor the people of Sodom. He politely explained his refusal by saying that he did not want anyone to think the king of Sodom had made him rich.

THOUGHTS FROM MOTHER SARAH

When my lord Abram told me what had transpired, I was stunned. The mysterious King Melchizedek was a representative of the invisible God who we both sincerely loved, worshipped, and served. It thrilled me that he met my lord. I was so glad that my lord gave to Melchizedek a portion of the spoils that he won in the war. God has so richly blessed us with material goods, so I was happy to give some back to him through the king of Salem.

But what I was even more interested in was the blessing King Melchizedek gave to my lord. I hope that his blessing will soon include a child for me. In giving 10 percent of what he had to God's service, my lord set an example for you, my dear daughters. I encourage you, out of your love and gratefulness to God, to do the same with your money.

BECOMING A FRIEND OF GOD

The two persons Abram met are figurative of the characters who have who influence us daily too. Melchizedek represents a man of God who is ready to congratulate us, encourage us, and rejoice in the greatness of God. The king of Sodom represents Satan, who is ready at every opportunity to steal our victory, minimize our joy, and cause further chaos and destruction. To defeat the suggestions and attacks of Satan in our lives, we vitally need godly influences. We see this with Melchizedek and Abram. Melchizedek, when he addressed Abram, referred to God twice as "the most high God" (verses 19 and 20). Afterwards, when Abram spoke with the king of Sodom, he, too, used the phrase "the most high God."

Godly influences and encounters are necessary in our own Christian lives. Melchizedek, besides the blessings that he gave to Abram, strengthened Abram and pointed to their God. Your pastor and your Christian friends encourage, congratulate, and influence you to serve God better. Your church is led by your pastor, a man of God doing the service of God. He is like Melchizedek and is worthy to receive a portion of your income.

The gift that Abram gave to Melchizedek, and Melchizedek to Abram, was very personal. We live in a time when we can financially support the work of God anywhere in the world with a click of a button. This can be a good thing, but it is also rather impersonal. Abram and Melchizedek met face-to-face and gave and received gifts. You should direct your financial giving toward places where you also get personal, face-to-face attention and help for your spiritual life.

While supporting ministries across the globe brings God glory, don't allow your global giving to deny your own church and pastoral team. They see you (hopefully!) on a weekly basis and generously spend time praying for you and giving attention to your needs. These people support you, so if you are going to financially give to the work of God, start with your own church leadership team who know and care for your spiritual welfare.

Words from Abraham's God

Malachi 3:10 Bring ye all the tithes into the storehouse, that there may be meat in mine house, and prove me now herewith, saith the LORD of hosts, if I will not open you the windows of heaven, and pour you out a blessing, that there shall not be room enough to receive it.

2 Corinthians 9:7 Every man according as he purposeth in his heart, so let him give; not grudgingly, or of necessity: for God loveth a cheerful giver.

1 Timothy 6:6 Godliness with contentment is great gain.

Hebrews 7:1-2 For this Melchisedec, king of Salem, priest of the Most High God, who met Abraham returning from the slaughter of the kings, and blessed him; To whom also Abraham gave a tenth part of all; first being by interpretation King of righteousness, and after that also King of Salem, which is, King of peace.

Hebrews 10:24 Let us consider one another to provoke unto love and to good works.

Prayer

Dear heavenly Father, it is out of great gratitude that I come before You today. You have given me so much. The money that You allow me to earn is only because of Your blessing to me.

Because of You, I have a mind and a body made to work and a source of income. It is only fitting that I should, out of gratitude to You, give back to You. But I realize You own everything, and my offering is so small. Yet it is with joy that I offer to Your work some of the material blessings You have allowed me to receive. This is part of my thanksgiving to You.

I pray that as I give to Your work that You will multiply my simple gifts for Your eternal glory. I ask this in the name of Your precious Son, Christ Jesus, amen.

Abram Considers the Stars

BIBLE READING — GENESIS 15: 1–6

LEARNING ABOUT FATHER ABRAHAM: After Abram chased Chedorlaomer's army out of the land and returned home, he may have been afraid of a future retaliation that would threaten either the land and/or himself, despite his recent military victory. God appeared to His concerned friend to comfort and encourage him and give him a glimpse of future blessings. God said that He would protect Abram Himself—be his shield and reward. Immediately upon hearing the word "reward," Abram voiced to God, in a thinly veiled complaint, that the one reward he so wanted more than anything else was a child, an heir of his very own. Without children, the aging Abram believed that his accumulated wealth would have to be left to one of his servants, and this idea did not please him.

Gently, God gave Abram additional, specific information. He told Abram that he would have a child produced from his own body. Then God led Abram outside and told him to look at the stars. God asked Abram a rhetorical question: could he count all the stars? While Abram was considering the multitude of the stars in the universe (perhaps he started to count them), God told him that his offspring would be as many as the stars—uncountable. This was a twofold promise to Abram: that he was going to have his own biological children and also innumerable spiritual children. God had told him before that his physical descendants would be as many as the grains of sand in the world, but not that he would have spiritual descendants too.

Perhaps Abram realized that his servant Eliezer, and his other servants, whom he had taught to worship God, were some of his first spiritual children. But when he looked at the stars, he must have had a glimpse of how great God's promise was.

Scientists have estimated that there are more stars in the universe than there are grains of sand on the earth. The heavenly body of a star, although tiny when viewed at such a distance, is so much greater and magnificent than a grain of sand! Abram did not understand, nor could he comprehend, the enormity of his glorious reward. He simply believed what God told him! Abram had no more questions and certainly no more complaints. He was most likely speechless, but he accepted God's words with joy. This simple belief on Abram's part was a righteous act.

THOUGHTS FROM MOTHER SARAH

When my lord told me that God had appeared to him again and told him we would have a child, I was confused and even sad because I was more than seventy years old! But I was intrigued and cautiously thrilled with the thought of spiritual children. I knew my lord was careful to teach our servants about his friend, and to lead them in worship of our creator. It gave me great joy to know that our servants loved our God too.

My dear daughter, when God showed my lord Abram the stars in the sky representing spiritual children to come, one of those stars that night represented you! Long before you had a physical birth, you were thought of and loved by God and by us, even though we did not understand. You are a very special woman. As one of my daughters, seek to share your love and your knowledge about our God with others so that you will have the blessing of spiritual children as well.

BECOMING A FRIEND OF GOD

When Abram was afraid, God's message comforted him. Many times, we, too, are afraid. So many times, we want God to talk with us audibly and directly, and give us words of comfort and encouragement and a glimpse of future blessings. Although we may sometimes envy Abram hearing God's audible voice, unlike Abram (who had to wait to hear from God), we always have God's promises at our fingertips in the form of our Bible. Our completed Bible, God's Word, is a far greater treasure than the few words Abram had.

The command of God to Abram in Genesis 15, where He says "Fear not," is the first of sixty "fear nots" in the Bible. Although these words were addressed specifically to other people in other situations, God recorded them in the Bible as a comforting order to us also.

Abram was concerned about his physical future. God not only gave him a promise about this, but He also directed Abram's focus to something far greater—a spiritual future.

The conversation between Abram and God gives us both comfort and insight. While we are in this physical world ("at home in the body," as the apostle Paul tells us in 2 Corinthians 5:6), we, like Abram, have physical concerns. While God understands this and provides for us physically, He wanted Abram to get a glimmer of understanding about spiritual blessings. The spiritual blessings in the spiritual world of the future, vastly downsized into the simple word "heaven," are far greater and indescribably more wonderful than what we can ever imagine. But, like Abram, we must simply believe God's words to us as a righteous act on our part.

We, too, can have spiritual children. While we women have limited ability to produce physical children, the number of our spiritual children can be unlimited. The effort that you put forth in witnessing, teaching, and praying will yield significant and eternal results that you cannot see or even appreciate presently, yet they will bring you unspeakable joy and spiritual children throughout eternity.

Words from Abraham's God

Psalm 28:7 The LORD is my strength and my shield; my heart trusted in him, and I am helped: therefore my heart greatly rejoiceth; and with my song will I praise him.

Isaiah 41:8 Thou, Israel, art my servant, Jacob whom I have chosen, the seed of Abraham my friend.

Galatians 3:29 If ye be Christ's, then are ye Abraham's seed, and heirs according to the promise.

Hebrews 11:6 Without faith it is impossible to please him: for he that cometh to God must believe that he is, and that he is a rewarder of them that diligently seek him.

1 Peter 3:6 Even as Sara obeyed Abraham, calling him lord: whose daughters ye are, as long as ye do well, and are not afraid with any amazement.

Prayer

Dear heavenly Father, thank You for providing for all my physical needs and even for my desires. You are so good to me in this world, and I have learned to trust You.

Because of Your great goodness to me now, I look forward with great anticipation to all the blessings You will give me once I am finally in Your presence. Like Abram, I am in awe of all the great blessings that You have reserved for me. I can only simply thank, praise, and glorify You humbly and sincerely. I give You my thanks through Your precious Son, Christ Jesus. Amen.

God's Covenant with Abram

BIBLE READING — GENESIS 15: 7–21

LEARNING ABOUT FATHER ABRAHAM: In this passage of Scripture, the LORD established His covenant with Abram both visually and verbally. After God told Abram that he would inherit the land where he was living, Abram asked God the obvious question: "How will I know this?" God's answer to Abram was with instructions to offer Him a sacrifice. This sacrifice used specific animals: a heifer, a female goat, and a ram, plus two different species of birds—a turtledove and a pigeon.

All the non-fowl animals were exactly three years old—at the peak of their mature usefulness. Abram prepared these animals for sacrifice and waited. The specific instructions from God about this special sacrifice taught Abram that the sacrificial animals represented something about the promised seed of the woman. Abram may have realized the seed promised to Adam and Eve was going to be God's perfect sacrifice.

After Abram prepared his sacrifice, birds of prey tried to eat the dead animals, but Abram chased the invading birds away to protect what he was offering to God. When sundown came, Abram fell into a deep sleep and was surrounded by great darkness. This darkness was clearly God because the pronoun "He" in verse 15 can only refer to God—only God was able to tell Abram what his future held, specifically regarding his offspring. God told Abram that his children would be strangers and afflicted servants in a foreign land for four hundred years, but God would deliver them in the fourth generation. Abram's children would then return and possess the land where he currently lived. God also promised that He would judge the nation that would afflict Abram's seed and that He would bring out his descendants "with great substance." Lastly, God told Abram that he would live long and die peacefully.

Then Abram saw both a smoking furnace and a burning lamp pass between the severed pieces of carcass. These two heat-producing objects were both manifestations of God Himself (see Exodus 13:21), showing that God had accepted Abram's sacrifice. God passed through the pieces of the sacrifice to show Abram that He was binding Himself to fulfill the promises He had just made. God Himself would bring them to pass. There was nothing Abram could do that would nullify God's promised blessing, both to him directly and to his future children.

BECOMING A FRIEND OF GOD

God always requires some sort of sacrifice. Long ago, God asked Abram to sacrifice living animals. Today, God asks us, His people, to be a living sacrifice—to give Him our body and mind—to bring glory to Him. The sacrificial animals in Abram's day represented, and pointed toward, the ultimate sacrifice of Jesus on the cross.

The birds that attempted to eat the carcasses symbolized the attacks of Satan, "the fiery darts of the wicked" (Ephesians 6:16), who tries to hinder and steal the joy of our service to God. As Abram had to protect his offering to God, we also need to protect what God has given us. Protection is a vital part of our Christian life. Satan can and will use anything to hinder our service and try to destroy our lives and our testimony. Knowing this is vital. We Christian women must guard our private times of prayer and Bible reading; we must also protect our habit of public worship, of regularly being in God's house, and of doing our part in protecting the ministry of our local church.

Sometimes we need to protect ourselves from toxic people. There are people, it seems, whose sole purpose in life is to cause problems, steal the joy of others, or simply become an emotional drain on others' time and energy. You need to protect yourself from these people or else you will become useless to both God and everyone around you.

Protecting yourself from the attacks of Satan, no matter what form they present themselves in, is a necessary part of your daily Christian life. It is important to ask for God's help every day, and for His protection over all that He has given you. Learn to protect those things you value with your own wise actions.

THOUGHTS FROM MOTHER SARAH

When my lord told me about his latest experience with God, I was afraid! In fact, for many nights afterward, my lord was hesitant to go to sleep because although we know God is our friend, He is a fearful, magnificent, mighty being. I rejoiced that this powerful God favored my lord with such great and wonderful promises. By this time, I had concluded that although, somehow, my lord would have children, I was past hope of bearing a child. I comforted myself with the thought that at least my lord would become a father, and I was determined to be happy for him. My dear daughter, always seek spiritual blessings for your husband and encourage him to have a closer relationship with our God.

Words from Abraham's God

Exodus 3:17 I have said, I will bring you up out of the affliction of Egypt unto the land of the Canaanites, and the Hittites, and the Amorites, and the Perizzites, and the Hivites, and the Jebusites, unto a land flowing with milk and honey.

1 Kings 8:12 Then spake Solomon, The LORD said that he would dwell in the thick darkness.

Psalm 18:11 He [God] made darkness his secret place; his pavilion round about him were dark waters and thick clouds of the skies.

Acts 7:6 God spake [to Abram] on this wise, that his seed should sojourn in a strange land; and that they should bring them into bondage, and entreat them evil four hundred years.

Romans 12:1 I beseech you therefore, brethren, by the mercies of God, that ye present your bodies a living sacrifice, holy, acceptable unto God, which is your reasonable service.

Hebrews 6:13 When God made promise to Abraham, because he could swear by no greater, he sware by himself.

Prayer

Dear heavenly Father, You are such a powerful being, yet You care about me and You want the very best for me. I am in awe of Your love and concern for me. Since You are so great and wonderful, help me to daily offer myself to Your service. As I attempt to serve You, I need Your protection from the wiles and attacks of the devil, no matter what form they may present themselves in. Please give me great wisdom and Your protection of my spiritual service to You and all You have blessed me with. Help me use myself as Your excellent servant. I am asking these things in the name of Your precious Son, the perfect sacrifice, Christ Jesus, amen.

Abram, Sarai, and the Surrogate Mother

BIBLE READING — GENESIS CHAPTER 16: 1–16

LEARNING ABOUT FATHER ABRAHAM: God had promised a son to Abram several times, which seemed to indicate that his wife Sarai would conceive; but Sarai was seventy-six years old and past menopause, seemingly physically unable to have a child. I use the word "seemingly" because Sarai said to her husband, "Behold now, the LORD hath restrained me from bearing" (v. 2). She didn't say she couldn't have a child because of her age, just that the LORD was keeping her from conception.

Sarai still longed to have a baby to raise, so she got the idea to give her Egyptian maid Hagar to Abram as his second wife, using Hagar's younger and fertile womb to bear Abram's child. Then Sarai could adopt and raise the infant and teach it to know, love, and worship their God. Abram agreed to this, and soon Hagar was carrying Abram's unborn son.

Sarai's suggestion resulted in Hagar being elevated from the lowly status of a servant to the expectant wife of a rich and respected nobleman. Then, knowing that she was carrying the child of her former mistress's husband, something Sarai seemed incapable of, Hagar became prideful and despised and scorned Sarai. When Sarai complained about this to Abram, Abram removed his protection as a husband to Hagar. He divorced her and demoted her to the position of Sarai's maid again. But Sarai was still jealous of her servant and, possibly, ashamed of her original idea to use Hagar as a surrogate mother. Sarai made life miserable for the pregnant Hagar, perhaps even secretly hoping that Hagar would miscarry.

Sarai's treatment of Hagar was so harsh that Hagar ran away. But God wasn't through with either Hagar or her unborn son. The angel of the LORD found her—rejected, homeless, and hopeless—near a well of water and instructed her to return to Sarai and submit to her. The angel also gave Hagar a great promise that God would multiply her offspring exceedingly. The angel then named her unborn son Ishmael, which means "the LORD hears."

Hagar, out of gratitude to God and His goodness, named the well *Beerlahairoi*, meaning "the well of him that lives and sees me." She had faith in the promise of the God of Abram and Sarai. Hagar obeyed the angel of the LORD and returned to Abram and Sarai. No doubt she told them what she had seen and heard.

When her son was born, Abram, at eighty-six years old, was finally a father. He named his firstborn son Ishmael. Ishmael eventually became the progenitor of the Arab nations—multitudes of people—as foretold by the angel.

As mentioned before, Hagar named the place of life-giving water *Beerlahairoi*. This name is a foreshadow of the Holy Spirit, the Spirit of God, the living God who sees all, and He is represented many times in Scriptures by water.

THOUGHTS FROM MOTHER SARAH

I used her and then afterwards I abused her. I am so embarrassed of myself, and I wish I could hide my shameful actions from you, my dear daughter. But since I cannot, the best I can do is counsel you to learn from my lack of faith and ensure you don't make a similar mistake.

Many men had multiple wives, but my lord never did. He said that he followed the pattern of our first father, Adam. God only gave him mother Eve, and my lord knew that one man for one woman was God's plan for families. But my idea to use Hagar's body created heartbreak for us, and Ishmael was not a surrogate child for me. Seeing little Ishmael made me feel even emptier than before.

Please, dear daughter, don't get impatient with God. Before you try and help God out, remember my mistake and how I lived to regret it.

BECOMING A FRIEND OF GOD

You may find yourself in a place like Hagar's. She was a victim of circumstance and a broken woman, but regardless of those things, Hagar was still a woman of faith. No matter what happened to you that made you feel broken and rejected, God sees you, no matter where you are. He wants you to look to Him for direction and instruction. As with Hagar, God has a message and plans for you. Be willing to listen, take Him at His word, and obey His commands. God cares enough about you to seek you out. Thank Him for that and seek to determine His will for your life.

Words from Abraham's God

Psalm 142:5 I cried unto thee, O LORD: I said, Thou art my refuge and my portion in the land of the living.

Proverbs 14:12; 16:25 There is a way which seemeth right unto a man, but the end thereof are the ways of death.

John 4:10 Jesus answered and said unto her, If thou knewest the gift of God, and who it is that saith to thee, Give me to drink; thou wouldest have asked of him, and he would have given thee living water.

Galatians 4:22 It is written, that Abraham had two sons, the one by a bondmaid, the other by a freewoman.

1 Peter 2:18 Servants, be subject to your masters with all fear; not only to the good and gentle, but also to the froward.

Prayer

Dear heavenly Father, help me to not be like Abram and Sarai and run ahead of You. Help me trust in You, even in hard times. Help me to be obedient to You even when You tell me to do difficult things. Help me rest in Your timing. Thank You for caring for me. While others may have done wrong to me, I believe You care for me and that I am special to You. Thank you for this. And help me to have more faith. In Christ's name I pray, amen.

Introducing Abraham

BIBLE READING — GENESIS 17:1–8

LEARNING ABOUT FATHER ABRAHAM: It had been more than a decade since God had last spoken to Abram. Abram was now ninety-nine years old, Sari was eighty-nine, and Abram's son Ishmael was thirteen. During the years Abram did not hear from God, it might have been in his mind that he had messed up beyond God's forgiveness regarding the situation with Ishmael and his mother, Hagar. Would God ever speak to him again? It's certain that Abram pondered all the things God had previously told him. While it is not mentioned in Scripture, we can assume that during those "silent years," Abram still worshipped daily and thought about all that God had told him and all that he knew about God. And then the LORD appeared to Abram again.

This time, God introduced Himself to Abram as *El Shaddai,* the Hebrew title for "the Almighty God." This title was to remind Abram of God's creative power and that there was nothing too hard for Him. This introduction was a foreshadowing of what God was about to do—something supernatural!

God commanded Abram to walk with Him and to be perfect. Perhaps this was a gentle rebuke referring to Abram's decision to father Ishmael. God reminded Abram of His covenant with him and His promise to give Abram children. Abram responded by falling on his face before God out of respect and worship of this mighty being who was also his friend.

Then God did something rather strange. He changed Abram's name to Abraham, which means "father of many nations." God injected the fifth Hebrew letter ה (pronounced "heh") into Abram's name. In the Hebrew language, each letter of the alphabet has its own meaning and ה means "breath" or "spirit." This name change was an outward expression of what God did both physically and spiritually to Abraham. God breathed His breath into Abraham's body, which gave him a new physical life that enabled him to physically become the father of many nations.

God then iterated His covenant with Abraham, telling him the nations of people he would father included prominent men and kings. God wanted a multitude of people to love and worship Him like Abraham—people who wanted to be friends of God. Abraham was to be the first of these special people. Also, these people would need a place to live, so God told Abraham that He was going to give the entire land of Canaan to Abraham's offspring as their everlasting possession.

THOUGHTS FROM MOTHER SARAH

I blamed myself for the birth of Ishmael. God had not spoken to my lord for years. I felt like the first mother Eve, who listened to the serpent, ate the forbidden fruit, and, as a result, was thrust out of paradise with Adam. When God did not speak to my lord, I felt it was because of my sinful acts. But although I wept bitter tears and resigned myself to never becoming a mother, my lord still encouraged me to daily worship God with him, despite God's silence.

My dear daughter, let me remind you that God is always good, and He always deserves your praise, your worship, and, yes, your obedience to Him—despite what He may allow in your life. Let me encourage you to worship God simply for who He is and not just because He can give you what you want.

BECOMING A FRIEND OF GOD

The name change of Abraham is like our change in present-day salvation. When we accept Jesus Christ as our Savior, God's Holy Spirit—His breath—fills us and changes us spiritually. With this inward change, God gives us, His children, great promises that are even greater than those given to His friend Abraham. Here are just a few of the great promises God has given to believers:

- A sound mind (2 Timothy 1:7)
- All things to inherit, not just a piece of land (Revelation 21:7)

- We become sons of God, not just friends (Galatians 4:6)

- A permanent sealing of God's Spirit, His presence, in us (Ephesians 1:13)

- The invitation to daily cast our cares on Him with the assurance that He cares for us (Peter 5:7)

- Direction for our lives (Proverbs 3:6)

- Eternal life with Him in heaven (John 14:3)

- Forgiveness of our sins (1 John 1:9)

- God's completed Word, the Bible. We don't have to wait to hear God; we have His words (Hebrews 4:12)

- Jesus intercedes to God for us (Hebrews 7:25)

Words from Abraham's God

Nehemiah 9:7 Thou art the LORD the God, who didst choose Abram, and broughtest him forth out of Ur of the Chaldees, and gavest him the name of Abraham.

Jeremiah 32:27 Behold, I am the LORD, the God of all flesh: is there any thing too hard for me?

Acts 7:5 [God] gave him [Abraham] none inheritance in it, no, not so much as to set his foot on: yet he promised that he would give it to him for a possession, and to his seed after him, when as yet he had no child.

2 Corinthians 5:17 If any man be in Christ, he is a new creature: old things are passed away; behold, all things are become new.

Hebrews 8:6 Now hath he obtained a more excellent ministry, by how much also he is the mediator of a better covenant, which was established upon better promises.

Prayer

Dear heavenly Father, thank You so much for Your promise of eternal life. When things are tough in my life, help me hold onto Your promises—all of them—knowing that You have the answers for me and that You and Your solutions transcend even this present life. Thank You for being my firm foundation.

Help me comfort myself in Your unchanging love and in all of Your wonderful promises in Your Holy Word! You thought of me so long ago and brought me into existence and then into favor with You, the God of all creation. You have given me such great and wonderful promises! I cannot fully imagine all of Your goodness to me, but I humbly thank You for Your great promises and accept them. I ask that somehow I could please You, so that I will glorify You. I humbly and sincerely worship You in the name of Your Son, Christ Jesus. Amen.

DAY 12

Circumcision, a Token of the Covenant

BIBLE READING — GENESIS 17: 9–14

LEARNING ABOUT FATHER ABRAHAM: God told His friend Abraham that he was going to be the father of multitudes of people God wanted to Him to love, and that his male offspring would have a special physical mark. His descendants were to be different from those of the heathen nations around them.

Just as God taught Adam and Eve the ritual of blood animal sacrifice and how to properly prepare an animal (Genesis 3:21, 4:4), God now instructed Abraham about circumcision. It would be a physical mark, a token that showed the spiritual promise that would identify Abraham's seed for generations. Every Jewish, male baby was to have his foreskin surgically removed at exactly eight days old. This permanent mark would be a mark of honor that would identify him as belonging to Abraham's household. It would also show that his parents accepted and embraced God's covenant. Even the non-related male servants and their sons who lived with Abraham were to be circumcised.

Abraham's servants were symbolically the first of Abraham's spiritual offspring, since he had instructed them in the ways and the worship of the LORD, and they showed their worship and allegiance toward the one true God by accepting the blood token of the promise between Abraham's offspring and God.

This procedure is so vitally important that any Hebrew who decided *not* to circumcise their son would be cut off from his people. While Bible scholars dispute the exact meaning of the phrase "cut off," the consequences of not obeying this act were severe, including death of the offender (Exodus 4:24–26).

After God instructed Abraham about circumcision, Abraham understood that shedding blood, the cutting away of excess flesh, was a vital part of his relationship with his God.

Abraham had to do what God commanded him. Immediately, he circumcised his thirteen-year-old son Ishmael, and all the male members of his household, before being circumcised himself at the age of ninety-nine. Despite his lack of faith in what God had promised to do for Sarah, Abraham did not hesitate to perform the bloody but necessary rite of circumcision.

THOUGHTS FROM MOTHER SARAH

When Abraham told me that God expected our men to be cut in their private and sensitive part, it appalled me! How could a loving God expect us to cut the flesh of our men, especially our tiny sons? But the more I thought and considered this, I understood.

It was common among the heathens to cut themselves and make permanent markings in their flesh as a reminder of various things—many times relating to departed loved ones or as part of their worship to their false gods. I understood why God wanted our males to be marked like this, yet I was very relieved and grateful that this command did not include women!

BECOMING A FRIEND OF GOD

Circumcision was a physical token in Old Testament times, a procedure instituted by God that made the men of God's culture different from the cultures around them. It was also, and still is, a reminder of a Jewish man's spiritual heritage. While circumcision today is still widely practiced, the reasons are more cultural and traditional and are sometimes chosen for health reasons rather than religious ones. But we can make an application from what was done physically to Old Testament males to something just as important in the Christian woman's life—her practice of daily devotions.

- Circumcision reminded the Jewish male daily that he was circumcised. Your devotional time should also be daily. Though there is no biblically set time to have devotions, meeting with God first thing in the morning is a good way to start your day (Psalm 5:3; Mark 1:35).

- Circumcision was physical but showed something spiritual. Your devotional time involves the physical act of reading and praying, but you are also performing a spiritual duty.

- Circumcision was permanent. Your devotional time should be a permanent part of your life. As long as you live, the acts of reading and hearing the Word of God and praying should be permanent parts of your daily routine.

- Circumcision is personal and so is your devotional time! While there is both a time and a place for public or family prayer and Bible reading, the Christian needs private time when he or she meets with God. No one else is allowed; your private time with God is personal. This is about you—*your* needs, *your* desires, *your* confession of *your* private sins to God, and *your* private worship of God.

Your time alone with God is a vital part of your Christian life. If you have not yet developed this spiritual and beneficial habit, today is a good time to start. If you already have personal devotions, then let this be a reminder of how necessary this practice with God is for your day-to-day Christian walk.

Words from Abraham's God

Psalm 5:3 My voice shalt thou hear in the morning, O LORD; in the morning will I direct my prayer unto thee, and will look up.

Luke 2:21 When eight days were accomplished for the circumcising of the child, his name was called Jesus, which was so named of the angel before he was conceived in the womb.

Romans 4:11 [Abraham] received the sign of circumcision, a seal of the righteousness of the faith which he had yet being uncircumcised: that he might be the father of all them that believe, though they be not circumcised; that righteousness might be imputed unto them also.

1 Corinthians 7:19 Circumcision is nothing, and uncircumcision is nothing, but the keeping of the commandments of God.

Galatians 6:15 In Christ Jesus neither circumcision availeth any thing, nor uncircumcision, but a new creature.

Prayer

Dear heavenly Father, thank You for desiring to meet with me every single day. Help me realize that my time with You is a very special and important appointment. My devotional time is not a magic ritual or a series of positive affirmations but a personal time for me to connect with You, my creator and my Savior. Help me guard this practice, protect it, and be faithful to meet with You.

Show me how to spiritually circumcise—cut off—anything that would hinder me from my special time of meeting with You. Show me that my time of Bible reading and prayer is not drudgery but a special time communing with my greatest friend. Let me hear Your voice and then, as I leave my burdens with You, let me be both energized and comforted so that I can be a blessing to others. I ask this in the name of Your Son, Christ Jesus. Amen.

Sarah and the Promise of Isaac

BIBLE READING — GENESIS 17:15–27

LEARNING ABOUT FATHER ABRAHAM: Along with Abram's name change to Abraham, God told Abraham that He was changing his wife's name from Sarai to Sarah, which means "princess," and that she would be blessed with a son. Sarah would also become the "mother of nations." "Princess" in this case was appropriate since this woman would become the great-grandmother of kings.

Abraham laughed at this incredible statement by God, knowing that he was one hundred years old and Sarah was ninety! Since Abraham did not have the faith to accept this incredible promise concerning his beloved but elderly Sarai, Abraham wanted Ishmael to receive the promised blessing instead.

God iterated what He had said. Abraham's elderly wife Sarah would bear a child. Furthermore, God named this yet unborn

67

son Isaac, meaning "laughter"—a reminder of Abraham's disbelieving laugh. God told Abraham that He would establish His covenant with this miracle child and with Isaac's offspring. But Abraham desired a blessing for Ishmael too, so God promised that Ishmael would father twelve princes that would also become a great nation. But God made it clear that He would establish His covenant with Isaac, not Ishmael. God then told Abraham that at the same time next year, Sarah would deliver their son.

THOUGHTS FROM MOTHER SARAH

It took me some time to get used to my new name, but being called Sarah made me feel different, healthier, and even younger than my ninety years. My lord assured me that God had said that within a year, I would be the biological mother of a son whose name would be Isaac, or "laughter." At age ninety, I would laugh with our newborn son! The very thought made me laugh, not joyfully but with bitterness. Sometimes, I wondered if my lord was truly hearing God's voice or if he was losing his mind.

If this was not bizarre enough, my lord had cut himself in his most private and sensitive area! I knew for sure that nothing would happen that would lead to my getting pregnant for at least the next several weeks. As if I could even have a child at my age!

My dear daughter, I did not believe God's promise, even though He had assured my lord that He would give me a child. Let me

*remind you that God always keeps His word, but He does not
always work in the timeframe and in the way we expect.*

BECOMING A FRIEND OF GOD

Humans are impatient creatures; we want things yesterday, at
the very latest. But God operates outside time. Although God
knows very well the limitations of our world, including time,
He does have His own will. While we must patiently learn to
wait on Him for answers to our heartfelt prayers and desires,
we also have the responsibility of being obedient to His
commands and doing His will. God is not our puppet. Rather,
we are His servants. We serve Him. Though He is good and
gracious and desires us to cast our cares upon Him, it is only
because of His goodness that we have all of the blessings we
enjoy. We are obligated to Him. He is not obligated to us.
Therefore, while we are waiting on Him, we must be obedient
in our service to Him.

While waiting is long, hard, and boring, this segment of
Abraham's and Sarah's life shows that God is not limited. He
has a perfect plan for us, which many times is far greater than
we can ask or imagine. While Abraham was willing to settle for
far less in having Ishmael receive the great blessing, God
wanted him to have a son with his beloved wife, a desire that
Sarah had had for a very long time. God has a way of working
things out, not only for our good but also for giving us far
more than we could imagine. The key is our steadfast trust in
Him and complete obedience to Him.

Also, there is an encouraging note in this passage of Scripture. Perhaps Sarah had given up on life; despite all of Abraham's riches, she had failed to have a child. She may have even been depressed and angry. But God had not given up on her. Despite her advanced age, God still had a job for her to do: to become a mother. Whatever age you may be reading this devotional, know that God has a purpose for your life. Thank Him for that and ask for His help in fulfilling His reasons for your existence.

Words from Abraham's God

Psalm 37:4 Delight thyself also in the LORD; and he shall give thee the desires of thine heart.

Psalm 62:5 My soul, wait thou only upon God; for my expectation is from him.

Psalm 92:14 They shall still bring forth fruit in old age; they shall be fat and flourishing.

Isaiah 54:1 Sing, O barren, thou that didst not bear; break forth into singing, and cry aloud, thou that didst not travail with child: for more are the children of the desolate than the children of the married wife, saith the LORD.

Isaiah 64:4 Since the beginning of the world men have not heard, nor perceived by the ear, neither hath the eye seen, O God, beside thee, what he hath prepared for him that waiteth for him.

Prayer

Dear heavenly Father, thank You for Your reminder to me that Your timing is not mine. Help me fill my days, even my years, with sincere service to You.

Help me realize that my life is not solely about me and what I want, even though You created me as a unique individual with specific and personal desires. As I share what I want with You, help me focus on You rather than on myself. And when You give me the desires of my heart, let me be careful to give You my sincere thanks because all my good and perfect gifts, all answers to my prayers, come from You alone. I ask this in Christ's name, amen.

The Visitors and Their Visit

BIBLE READING — GENESIS 18:1–15

LEARNING ABOUT FATHER ABRAHAM: Abraham was living in a tent on the plains of Mamre, close to the city of Sodom. It had been nearly three months since God had last spoken to him. One day, as he was trying to keep cool in the heat of the day and, perhaps, also expectantly waiting to hear from the LORD again, Abraham looked up and saw three men walking toward him.

Abraham, seeing the visitors, ran to meet them and humbly bowed down before them. Abraham suspected that one visitor was his friend, the LORD, accompanied by two angels. He offered his guests food, water, and rest. Abraham directed Sarah to make bread for them while he ran to the herd to get fresh meat to serve. Despite being one hundred years old, Abraham was literally running around! He had received the breath of God and was not feeble.

72

Abraham served his guests a meal, and after they finished eating, they asked Abraham about Sarah. Abraham told them that Sarah was in the tent. The LORD told Abraham that He would return to Abraham "according to the time of life" (nine months) and that Sarah would have a son!

Sarah heard this exchange and inwardly laughed in scorn and disbelief. She knew she was an old woman. She had given up on the idea of creating and raising a child with her husband. But the LORD heard her silent, inward, scornful laughter and her thoughts. He addressed her disbelief of her husband, knowing that Abraham, too, had his doubts about Sarah bearing a child. He asked Abraham the rhetorical question, "Is anything too hard for the LORD?" He immediately followed His question with the repeated, affirmative statement that "according to the time of life" (v. 14), He would return and Sarah would deliver a son.

Sarah, who heard that she was being discussed and fearful of the Lord who knew her inward thoughts, denied she laughed. She may have laughed to herself, but God did hear her.

THOUGHTS FROM MOTHER SARAH

I was so happy to see these men leave. I didn't mind entertaining, not at all, but when one got too personal, talking about my having a child and then knowing what I was thinking, I was both sad and scared. I was sad because my greatest desire was to enjoy the pleasure of making a child with my husband. I had put that away, despite my lord's silly talk about what he thought God had told him.

My dear daughters, meeting God is a fearful experience because He knows and remembers all. You, too, will meet God someday, and you will have to give an account for all your actions—the wise and good, the unwise and bad.

BECOMING A FRIEND OF GOD

Abraham was a busy man with a very large household. Yet despite his constant attention to his daily tasks, he was intent on waiting and watching for the LORD to come with further instructions regarding the promise of a son.

While the LORD has not explicitly promised us a son, He *has* promised that He will come back to take us to heaven. The promise of His coming, to be caught up to meet Him in the air (1 Thessalonians 4:17), is just as valid as the promise the LORD gave Abraham. While generations of Christians have passed away waiting for this promise to be fulfilled, each day brings us closer to Christ's return in the air.

But while our mind knows about this great promise, we Christian women must be like Abraham and be busy with the daily tasks that are continually before us. Jesus said, "Occupy till I come" (Luke 19:13). Whether we meet Christ through death, as most believers have done, or if we cheat death when Christ returns and plucks us off this world to take us alive into heaven, we still have work that needs to be done. Looking forward to being with Him for eternity and having Christ's imminent return on our minds—while raising our families, working our jobs, and enjoying times of recreation—shows our faith in Him.

Abraham showed that it was a great privilege to serve his friend, the LORD. This great man humbled himself to do the work of a servant and served a meal to his distinguished guests. It is truly a joy and a privilege to serve the God of creation.

Serving God is work, but God's commands are not grievous. Sometimes, as in the example of Abraham and Sarah, His commands are pleasurable! The gift of carnal pleasure to gain a far greater gift—a son—was a shocking but pleasant realization to the elderly Sarah.

Words from Abraham's God

Matthew 24:42 Watch therefore: for ye know not what hour your Lord doth come.

Romans 9:9 This is the word of promise, At this time will I come, and Sara shall have a son.

1 Thessalonians 4:16-17 The Lord himself shall descend from heaven with a shout, with the voice of the archangel, and with the trump of God: and the dead in Christ shall rise first: Then we which are alive and remain shall be caught up together with them in the clouds, to meet the Lord in the air: and so shall we ever be with the Lord.

Hebrews 13:2 Be not forgetful to entertain strangers: for thereby some have entertained angels unawares.

1 John 5:3 This is the love of God, that we keep his commandments: and his commandments are not grievous.

Prayer

Dear heavenly Father, You are such a good and great God! You have made me, blessed me, and given me eternal life. You desire my service to You too. You give me joy when I obey, and You have also promised me great blessings in eternity.

I am so privileged to have You as my Father! I eagerly look forward to finally meeting You face-to-face one day. You are the one who loves me so much more than I could ever imagine and who has made all these great things possible. Mere words cannot express my gratitude. I can't fully understand nor even appreciate all of Your love for me, but I joyfully embrace all the goodness You offer me.

I bow before You in humble, grateful, and joyful worship for who You are and for all You do for me. I give You my meager praise through Your Son, Christ Jesus, who made possible all Your goodness to me. Amen.

Abraham the

Intercessor

BIBLE READING — GENESIS 18:16–33

LEARNING ABOUT FATHER ABRAHAM: When it came time for the LORD to leave with the two angels, Abraham, as a polite host, went to see them on their way. The LORD spoke to His two companions and asked them if He should reveal to Abraham what He intended to do. While God did not need the advice of the angels, this brief dialogue showed the LORD contrasting the righteous (Abraham) with the wicked (the inhabitants of Sodom). The LORD told Abraham that because of the wickedness of Sodom, He intended to destroy the city.

The LORD said that He had heard the cry of the people of Sodom, and He wanted to check out the report personally. God knew exactly what was going on in Sodom, but He is still a merciful and a long-suffering God (Matthew 11:23) and wanted to give Abraham to chance to speak up for Sodom. The two other men then continued on their journey toward Sodom and left Abraham alone with the LORD. Abraham, no doubt thinking about his nephew Lot in that wicked city slated for divine destruction, took it upon himself to intercede for the righteous souls, specifically Lot and his family.

Abraham pleaded with the LORD to spare the city if He found fifty righteous souls there. While Abraham did not mention his nephew by name, he held fast to the belief that Lot was a righteous man and that Lot influenced others in the city toward godliness.

Once Abraham elicited assurance from God that He would not destroy the city if He found fifty righteous people in it, Abraham then pleaded for God to spare the city from destruction if there were fewer righteous persons—forty-five, then forty, then thirty, and then twenty. Abraham and God finally came to the agreement that if God found only ten righteous souls, He would spare the entire city from destruction.

Abraham, in his pleas, asked God six different times using six different numbers to spare the city of Sodom, and each time he always received an affirmative answer from the LORD.

Surely Abraham believed that finding a mere ten righteous souls would not be a hard task in such a large city. Abraham was content that he had done his duty and that God would not destroy the city. Then the LORD went on His way to seek the ten righteous souls in Sodom and Abraham returned home.

THOUGHTS FROM MOTHER SARAH

My mind was still trying to sort out all that had transpired with our lunch guests when my lord returned and told me that God was intending to destroy Sodom. I knew it was an exceedingly wicked place, but Lot and his family lived there. My lord assured me, though, that God promised him that if there were but only ten righteous people there, God would spare the city.

Lot, his wife, and their two unmarried girls accounted for only four people. And as for his married daughters, we believed Lot would have only allowed them to marry honorable men, so we came up with at least ten people who we believed were righteous. We also hoped that Lot would have influenced at least one or two other people for the Lord. I was so impressed with how my lord persevered in his bargaining with the LORD.

My dear daughters, let my lord be an example to you in your prayers. Don't give up asking God for what you want. He hears your prayers, and He is a merciful God.

BECOMING A FRIEND OF GOD

The communication of Abraham with God concerning Lot was, no doubt, a blessing to God. To plead with God for those we love is an honorable act. Prayer is an action word; it is a work of love toward those we care for. When we know the danger that others are facing and we petition God for them, prayer is an act of selfless love.

Abraham knew that Lot and his family were in danger of God's judgment. He knew it better than they did, and so he pleaded with God to spare them. As Christians, we know the coming judgment of God on unbelievers and understand the danger of that judgment far better than they do. It is our duty to plead with God for them and ask God to convict their hearts so that they will repent and turn to Him. As adults, and especially as parents, we understand the perils that threaten harm on the lives of young people. Again, it is our duty to pray to God and ask for His protecting hand upon them.

Abraham spoke frankly but respectfully to his God, His friend. So, too, should we address God in our prayers. It is also beneficial when we pray to remind God of His attributes because He is good. This is a prayer of praise. We can also remind Him of His promises in His Word and claim them for ourselves, both as we intercede for ourselves and as we pray for our loved ones.

We don't always know how God uses our prayers to help those we care about, and we may not know until eternity, but we know that prayer moves the hand of God (Isaiah 59:1). While our loved ones have their own free will and have the privilege to make their own good or bad choices, if we don't pray for them when we see a need, then we have sinned against God (1 Samuel 12:23).

Words from Abraham's God

Isaiah 59:1 Behold, the LORD's hand is not shortened, that it cannot save; neither his ear heavy, that it cannot hear.

Amos 3:7 Surely the Lord GOD will do nothing, but he revealeth his secret unto his servants the prophets.

1 Samuel 12:23 God forbid that I should sin against the LORD in ceasing to pray for you: but I will teach you the good and the right way.

Ephesians 6:18 Praying always with all prayer and supplication in the Spirit, and watching thereunto with all perseverance and supplication for all saints.

James 5:16 Confess your faults one to another, and pray one for another, that ye may be healed. The effectual fervent prayer of a righteous man availeth much.

Prayer

Dear heavenly Father, prayer is work, hard work, and sometimes it is a task I don't want to do. Many times, when I don't see Your answers right away, I want to stop praying, and sometimes I do. Yet I know You delight in hearing me pray because, if nothing else, it is communication with You.

Thank You for the example of Your dear Son praying to You. Help me be faithful in praying to You, not only for myself but also for the needs of others. You are the source of all my blessings, and there is none like You.

I am humbled and grateful that You make Yourself available to me through prayer. To commune with You, the God of all creation, is a precious and wonderful privilege. Thank you for this wonderful blessing, in Jesus's name, amen.

The Story of Lot

BIBLE READING — GENESIS 19

LEARNING ABOUT FATHER ABRAHAM: The sobering
account of Abraham's nephew, Lot, and his family (Genesis 19)
might have been told to Abraham by Lot himself, months after
God destroyed the city of Sodom. After the angels departed
from Abraham and the LORD, they went to Sodom, where they
found Lot sitting at the gate—a place of prominence in the city.
When Lot saw the men, he bowed in respect, and he invited
them into his house for the night. Lot seemed to recognize that
there was something special and extraordinary about these two
men. The men, after initially rejecting Lot's offer of lodging,
accepted Lot's hospitality and ate the feast that Lot personally
prepared for them.

While they were eating, the news of these strangers staying
with Lot spread throughout the city. The men of Sodom, of all
ages, came from all parts of the city and insisted that Lot bring
out his special visitors so they could use them for their own
sinful pleasures—"that we may know them." Lot, not wanting
this to happen, left his house to reason with the men of
Sodom—whom he referred to as "brethren"—and warned

them not to do this wickedness. As a compromise, instead of his two male visitors, Lot offered his two, young, virgin daughters to these lust-crazed men to do with as they wished. But the men refused Lot's sacrificial offer and almost broke down the door of Lot's house trying to get at the visiting angels.

The crowd of men trying to get past Lot to the angels conferred among themselves and said that "this fellow," meaning Lot, chose to make his home in their city of his own free will. Because of that, they took offense that Lot had the audacity to confront the men concerning what they wanted to do with his visitors! About Lot they also said, "He will needs be a judge…" which can be interpreted as "Who does this stranger think he is that he would question us and deny us what we want?"

Angered that Lot would even hesitate to deliver his guests to them, they threatened to treat Lot even more severely than the angels. With Lot outside, and the commotion quickly escalating, the men of Sodom began to push against Lot at the door of his house. At that, the angels pulled Lot to safety inside his house and then struck the men of the city with blindness. Even with their sight gone, the men of Sodom wearied themselves trying to find the door of Lot's house to get at his angelic visitors.

While the blinded men of Sodom were still trying to get into Lot's house, the angels told Lot that God was going to destroy the city, and they urged him to gather his extended family and leave Sodom. Lot went to his married daughters' homes and urged his sons-in-law to flee the city and escape God's coming judgment. However, his sons-in-law treated both the news and Lot like a joke.

When morning came, the angels told Lot it was time to leave, but he lingered. Finally, because of the LORD's mercy, the angels took Lot, his wife, and their two daughters by the hand and firmly escorted them out of the city. Then the angels gave them explicit instructions to escape to the mountain and not look back, warning them that if they looked back, they, too, would be destroyed. Lot resisted and begged the angels to let him and his family go to the small city of Zoar instead of the mountain, and the angels agreed to his request. Although Zoar was also slated for destruction, the city would end up being spared for Lot's sake.

That morning, as soon as Lot entered Zoar, the Bible says the LORD rained brimstone and fire upon Sodom, Gomorrah, Admah, and Zeboim—all the cities of the plain excluding Zoar. But Lot's wife, despising the angels' warning, looked back toward Sodom and was turned into a pillar of salt.

The inhabitants of Zoar did not welcome Lot and his two daughters. In fact, seeing the judgment that fell upon their neighboring cities and that a woman in their midst had just been turned into a pillar of salt, they were scared out of their minds. Lot, fearing the evil countenances of the citizens of Zoar, ended up doing what the angels instructed in the first place—he went to the mountain.

However, while living in a mountain cave, Lot's two daughters, fearing they would never have children because all the men in their world were dead, came up with an idea straight from Sodom. First, they got their dad drunk with wine and then each daughter took her turn having sex with their father. As a result, Lot fathered a son with each of his daughters. This is the last time in the book of Genesis that Lot is mentioned.

THOUGHTS FROM MOTHER SARAH

The smell of sulfur awoke us. Looking out over the plain, we saw the flames where the city of Sodom and the other towns had been. Our first thought was of Lot and his family, which was quickly followed by the awful realization that there were not even ten righteous people found in the entire city! It was not until months later that Abraham finally met up with Lot and learned exactly what had happened on that fateful day.

As sad as Lot's ending was, he knew he could blame only himself. My lord had rescued his nephew once before, but Lot had insisted on staying in the wicked city of Sodom and made friends with the sinful people there. The influences of the wickedness of Sodom were so great on both Lot and his girls that they committed regrettable deeds from which there was no escape.

My dear daughter, I urge you to choose your friends wisely and to cultivate friendships with only godly people for your own good. God is long-suffering, and He gives second chances. But there comes a time when God allows us to reap the consequences of our own willful acts.

BECOMING A FRIEND OF GOD

This sobering account of God's judgment and mercy is a reminder to us. God showed mercy to Lot for the sake of His friend Abraham. Notwithstanding, this account also shows us God's gracious gift of free will.

God offered His mercy to Lot, his wife, his daughters—married and unmarried, his sons-in-law, plus any grandchildren he may have had, all because of the intercession of Abraham. It was not God's fault that so many of Lot's family perished. God gave them fair warning, and He sent angels to help them escape. Today, God freely offers his gift of salvation through His Son, the Lord Jesus Christ, to escape hell. Just as Lot's family members made their choices, so also do people today. A holy God must punish sin, but this same God is also merciful and offers an escape from His judgment. But only those who accept His offer on His terms will escape eternal damnation.

Words from Abraham's God

Romans 1:27 The men, leaving the natural use of the woman, burned in their lust one toward another; men with men working that which is unseemly, and receiving in themselves that recompence of their error which was meet.

Luke 17:28-29 As it was in the days of Lot; they did eat, they drank, they bought, they sold, they planted, they builded; But the same day that Lot went out of Sodom it rained fire and brimstone from heaven, and destroyed them all.

Luke 17:32 Remember Lot's wife.

2 Peter 2:7–8 [If God] delivered [righteous] Lot, vexed with the filthy conversation of the wicked: (for that righteous man dwelling among them, in seeing and hearing, vexed his righteous soul from day to day with their unlawful deeds;) the Lord knoweth how to deliver the godly out of temptations.

Jude 1:7 Even as Sodom and Gomorrah, and the cities about them in like manner, giving themselves over to fornication, and going after strange flesh, are set forth for an example, suffering the vengeance of eternal fire.

Prayer

Dear heavenly Father, thank You for Your mercy that You so freely offer to all. Thank You for saving me from hell that I, as a sinner, deserve. Help me now to share Your message of salvation with others because You love them too.

Keep me away from evil influences so that my soul does not get vexed and I suffer for it. Rather, help me surround myself with good people who will draw me closer, and help me love and serve You better. I ask this in the name of Your precious Son, Christ Jesus. Amen.

The Incident with Abimelech

BIBLE READING — GENESIS CHAPTER 20

LEARNING ABOUT FATHER ABRAHAM: After the destruction of Sodom, Abraham moved south and made his home in Gerar, a Philistine town. In Gerar, Abraham, as with Pharaoh years earlier (because he was afraid that the men of that place would kill him to possess his almost ninety-year-old, but strikingly beautiful wife Sarah), declared that Sarah was his sister. The king of Gerar (identified as Abimelech, a title—not a first name) wanted Sarah. Since she was proclaimed as being a single woman, Abimelech took her with the intention of making her his wife. However, God intervened and told Abimelech in a dream that Sarah was Abraham's wife.

Abimelech, shocked, told God that he took Sarah in pure innocence because Sarah had said that Abraham was her brother, not her husband. God told Abimelech that because he had taken Sarah in innocence, He had prevented him from having any intimate relationship with her. God instructed Abimelech to return Sarah back to her husband, who, He declared, was a prophet. God also warned Abimelech that if he did not return Sarah untouched, God would kill him and everyone in his house.

Abimelech, being a bit shaken by his dream, got up early the next morning and told his servants what had transpired. Then he strongly rebuked Abraham and told him "Thou hast done deeds unto me that ought not to be done" (v. 9). Abraham, to defend his deception, explained that he was in a place with people who did not fear God, which made him fear for his life. Then he let Abimelech know Sarah was indeed his half-sister, but he was married to her.

As an apology to Abraham for taking Sarah, Abimelech gave Abraham livestock, servants, and one thousand pieces of silver and returned Sarah to him. Abimelech then rebuked Sarah for her part in Abraham's deception. Lastly, Abimelech offered Abraham and Sarah the choice to live anywhere in his kingdom. While Sarah was in Abimelech's house, God prevented the women of his house from being able to conceive children, but after Sarah's return to her husband, Abraham prayed for Abimelech and the women's healing, and God allowed them to conceive children again.

THOUGHTS FROM MOTHER SARAH

This heathen king taught both my lord and me that my lord was a "covering of the eyes." I was honored that at age eighty-nine, I was still very desirable to men. But had the king realized I was a married woman, he would not have looked at me as a potential wife.

My daughter, your husband is a protection, a pause, and a barrier from other men looking too closely at you and desiring you for themselves. While you may be an extremely attractive woman, when other men know you are married, they realize you are off limits to them. When you reference your husband in your speech and wear your wedding ring, it makes those men look elsewhere for a wife, thus protecting your marriage.

I felt humiliated that it took a heathen king to teach us this lesson. And as much as it grieves me to admit it, my lord, especially, needed to hear this because it was his idea that I, again, pose as his sister. He thought to protect me, but he was not thinking of the danger it would put me in. My lord said that I would still have a child, so obviously God would not allow either one of us to die, but still. . . .

BECOMING A FRIEND OF GOD

This account in the life of Abraham is a good example of how to handle a situation when you get off track in your service to God. Sin, in the form of not trusting God, can and does happen to the best of us, but how we respond to correction is an important part of our Christian life and service. While there is no excuse for not trusting God and for taking things into our own hands, how we respond to that correction tells others much about our character.

A wise person will accept the rebuke, turn from his mistake (repent), and get back on track in serving God. Whether you have been away from God for just a single transgression or wasted many years in sinful self-will, God desires change in your heart, followed by a change in your actions.

This works also for past sins. You may have done something foolish or wrong in your past that you cannot undo and carry regret and guilt over. However, you do have today. If you have regrets in your life, sins that you committed, and failures that should not have happened, confess them all to God. Tell Him you regret what you did in the past. Tell Him that if you could go back with the knowledge you have now, you would do things differently. Then receive and accept His forgiveness, and with a clean, clear conscience, go on and serve Him the best that you can with the time and the opportunities He gives you. This is being a wise woman.

Words from Abraham's God

Psalm 32:5 I acknowledged my sin unto thee, and mine iniquity have I not hid. I said, I will confess my transgressions unto the LORD; and thou forgavest the iniquity of my sin. Selah.

Proverbs 9:8 Reprove not a scorner, lest he hate thee: rebuke a wise man, and he will love thee.

Proverbs 12:22 Lying lips are abomination to the LORD: but they that deal truly are his delight.

Proverbs 24:16 A just man falleth seven times, and riseth up again: but the wicked shall fall into mischief.

1 John 1:9 If we confess our sins, he is faithful and just to forgive us our sins, and to cleanse us from all unrighteousness.

Prayer

Dear heavenly Father, please help me to be sensitive when Your Spirit convicts me about my sin. I ask that you keep me from the personal failure of sinning against You; but when I do, please help me respond quickly to Your conviction, confess my failures to You, and then immediately look for opportunities to serve You again.

Help me have an even greater love for my husband because he is the protector of our marriage and family. Help my husband to trust God in a fuller and deeper way so that he can lead our family to do what is right before You. I thank You for this lesson and make these requests in the name of Christ Jesus. Amen.

Welcome, Baby Isaac!

BIBLE READING — GENESIS 21:1–8

LEARNING ABOUT FATHER ABRAHAM: In Genesis 20, the LORD closed the wombs of the women in Abimelech's house until Abraham prayed for them, but he opened the aged womb of Sarah. She conceived and gave birth to their son, Isaac, exactly when God said she would. After waiting for nearly a quarter of a century, the day that Sarah and Abraham had prayed for, dreamed about, and imagined (but given up on ever experiencing) was now a joyful reality. The years of waiting and the advanced ages of both parents were a clear testimony of God's power—ninety-year-old women with one hundred-year-old husbands don't have babies!

After Sarah delivered their son, Abraham followed God's commands and named his son Isaac, meaning "laughter." This Hebrew word has the connotation of indicating a scornful, snide type of laugher—not the happy, funny kind. This child's name was a constant reminder that humans should not scornfully laugh at their all-powerful creator. Then, exactly eight days after Isaac was born, Abraham took a sharp knife and circumcised his infant son, just as God had commanded him to do.

Sarah laughed with joy at the birth of Isaac. But when she held this miracle child, she also laughed at her own unbelief and lack of faith in not trusting that God could and would do what He had promised. Sarah nursed her newborn son, and he thrived and grew. Eventually, he was old enough to be weaned. To celebrate the transition from baby to young child, Abraham put on a grand feast for his son, no doubt inviting all his friends and neighbors to praise the LORD for His goodness.

THOUGHTS FROM MOTHER SARAH

I had laughed in scorn, thinking that this wonderful day and this perfect child, my own biological baby I waited so long for would ever be a reality! But he finally came—my Isaac—my joyful laughter! He was such a happy baby, always smiling and, yes, laughing.

Only God, our creator, my lord's friend, could do such a wonderful thing with my body. My dear daughter, it was hard for me to wait and desire a baby for all those years, but despite my unbelief and lack of faith, God kept His promise.

God wanted everyone, not only our neighbors and friends but also generations to come (including you, my dear daughter) to know that Isaac was truly a very special child given by God Himself.

Whatever you are waiting on for God to do in your life, be patient. God is working. He is building your faith and He will answer your prayers. While I know it is difficult, and it can be easy to give up hope in God, let me encourage you to rest in God's promises during your time of waiting. God may be silent, but He is not absent.

BECOMING A FRIEND OF GOD

The same God who gave Abraham and Sarah a child after it was biologically impossible is the same promise-keeping God we have today. Abraham and Sarah were not the exceptions to God making and keeping His promises; God is still doing the same thing for us today.

As we read God's Word, He speaks to us. The promises in the Bible are for us to claim amidst life's problems. But as we see in the account of Isaac, God does not immediately give us the desired results.

When we ask God for something (knowing that He alone can answer our prayers) and claim the promises in His Word, it is up to God to answer us both in His time and in His way. Our requests to God do not fall on deaf ears. God delights in hearing from us, and He also delights in answering our prayers. When God does not answer our prayers at the time we ask—*and in the way we think He should!*—He is still lovingly working on our behalf. He is bringing about something far greater for us—even better than what we can ask or think!

Allow God the time to answer your requests and fulfill His promises in His time and how He sees best. Then when He answers, be careful to give Him the praise, thanks, and honor He deserves.

While we are waiting on God, we need to be like Abraham and meditate on God's Word. The hearing, reading, and thinking on what God has given us in His Word builds our faith, even as we wait on Him.

We often claim God's promises for our trials in this life, and well we should. But the greatest promise that we have from God is that He will deliver us—those who have accepted Him as our Savior—from hell and take our soul (the true essence of ourselves) to heaven with Him when we die. This wonderful promise of God comforts us when we contemplate death and also when we face the death of a believing loved one. As we see God being faithful in helping us, answering our prayers, and providing for us daily, let us be careful to thank and praise Him for all that we see and for all He is doing for us that we cannot see.

Words from Abraham's God

Psalm 37:4 Delight thyself also in the LORD; and he shall give thee the desires of thine heart.

Psalm 126:2 Then was our mouth filled with laughter, and our tongue with singing: then said they among the heathen, The LORD hath done great things for them.

Hebrews 11:11 Through faith also Sara herself received strength to conceive seed, and was delivered of a child when she was past age, because she judged him faithful who had promised.

Acts 7:8 He gave him the covenant of circumcision: and so Abraham begat Isaac, and circumcised him the eighth day.

James 1:17 Every good gift and every perfect gift is from above, and cometh down from the Father of lights, with whom is no variableness, neither shadow of turning.

Prayer

Dear heavenly Father, I thank You that I can trust You to keep all Your promises to me. Thank You for caring about me. Amidst the billions of humans, I am significant to You, Almighty God. This thought is so humbling and yet so great!

Thank You for both promising and providing life for me throughout eternity, a never-ending life with You where pleasures abound. Your promises to me are so wonderful that I cannot understand or appreciate them properly, but I claim them and I humbly bow in adoration to You for all of Your great and precious guarantees. I worship You through Your Son, Christ Jesus. Amen.

The Plight of Hagar and Ishmael

BIBLE READING — GENESIS 21:9 TO 21

LEARNING ABOUT FATHER ABRAHAM: At the feast that Abraham hosted when Isaac was weaned, Sarah noticed (and more likely than not, everyone else at the feast noticed too) that Abraham's first son, Ishmael, was ridiculing Isaac. Sarah was furious. At that point, Ishmael was a teenager—about fourteen years old when Isaac was born. Sarah, in her fury, went to her husband and told him to get rid of both Hagar and Ishmael. Now that the promised son was born, Sarah, being a possessive mother, didn't want the lesser son to have any inheritance and, I'm sure, any relationship with Isaac or Abraham. Sarah's anger and her demand grieved Abraham because he loved Ishmael. Despite the wrong way that Ismael came into the world (Genesis 16:1–3), Ishmael was Abraham's firstborn son, and he held a special place in Abraham's heart.

While Abraham was considering what to do, God intervened and spoke to him. The Bible uses the name "God" throughout this passage of Scripture, which relates the narrative about Hagar and Ishmael rather than the comforting title of "the LORD." This shows that the all-powerful God had His hand on Hagar and Ishmael, but *they* did not have a friendship with God. God affirmed Sarah's demand and told Abraham that it was time for both Hagar and Ishmael to leave. He again reminded Abraham that Isaac was the promised heir. However, God also assured Abraham that He would make Ishmael into a great nation because he was Abraham's son.

Despite Abraham's feelings, he got up early the next morning, gave Hagar a parting present of bread and water, and sent her and her son away. Hagar, for her part, did not seem to have any clear direction of a future destination. Homeless, mother and son wandered in the wilderness of Beersheba and eventually ran out of water. Discouraged, helpless, and dehydrated, Hagar left a weakened Ishmael under a shrub to shield him from the hot sun, but with a mother's love, she could not watch him suffer and die. She possibly told him he was to rest and wait for her while she looked for water. After leaving Ishmael, the distraught Hagar started weeping. Meanwhile, Ishmael, too, was crying out—whether for water, God's help, or his mother's presence, we don't know. But God heard his cry and sent one of His angels with a message to his distressed mother. He told her that God had heard Ishmael and she was to return to him, and he shared God's promise that Ishmael would become a great nation and would not die. God then directed Hagar to a water source where she could fill her bottle.

God was with Ishmael as he grew up, and he became an archer and married a woman from Egypt, his mother's homeland.

THOUGHTS FROM MOTHER SARAH

When I demanded that my lord cast out Hagar and Ishmael, I was so angry and so tired of putting up with them both, I didn't care if they lived or died. They had been with us for years, but they never wanted to worship God like we did. There was always constant but subtle tension between Hagar and me. I was so glad when they left; things were much more peaceful.

Years later, when we learned they'd both survived, I was glad. If either had perished, I would have felt guilty and blamed myself.

My precious daughter, peace in your home is vitally important, not only for your husband and children but also for your own soul. A woman sets the mood of her home, so I urge you to work to create and maintain a peaceful atmosphere.

BECOMING A FRIEND OF GOD

The Egyptian boy who mocked the promised son is a picture of unbelievers mocking both Christ and those who follow Him. The lure of the sinful pleasures of this world is strong, and it is easy to get attached to things that hinder our Christian testimony and service to Christ. Many times, we don't want to give up activities, friends, or habits that we know are wrong, especially when they feel so good.

When we realize we need to separate from ungodly influences or people, we immediately need to obey God and His Word, even when it grieves us. Our purpose in this life is to glorify God. Therefore, our recreation, our work, and our close companions need to be God honoring. When we refuse to separate ourselves from sinful influences, our peace with God will suffer, and so will our fellowship, service, and prayers to God.

Sometimes we may find ourselves in a position like Hagar's and drown in self-pity, even if the reason is a good one. In that case, the message from God, delivered by the angel, applies to us today. In short, stop looking at yourself and instead help someone else who is in a worse situation. Getting involved in helping others is a sure cure for depression. There is no better help than to take and share "the water of the word" (Ephesians 5:26) with those who are spiritually dying and desperately in need of it. That message can deliver them from eternal death.

Words from Abraham's God

John 15:19 If ye were of the world, the world would love his own: but because ye are not of the world, but I have chosen you out of the world, therefore the world hateth you.

Galatians 4:29–30 As then he that was born after the flesh persecuted him that was born after the Spirit, even so it is now. Nevertheless what saith the scripture? Cast out the bondwoman and her son: for the son of the bondwoman shall not be heir with the son of the freewoman.

Hebrews 11:18 Of whom it was said, That in Isaac shall thy seed be called.

James 4:4 Ye adulterers and adulteresses, know ye not that the friendship of the world is enmity with God? whosoever therefore will be a friend of the world is the enemy of God.

1 John 2:15–16 Love not the world, neither the things that are in the world. If any man love the world, the love of the Father is not in him. For all that is in the world, the lust of the flesh, and the lust of the eyes, and the pride of life, is not of the Father, but is of the world.

Prayer

Dear heavenly Father, help me as I strive to create peace in my home, but to do that, I must have peace with You. Help me remove sinful pleasures that, although enjoyable for a season, interfere with my relationship with You. When I am out of fellowship with You, then I am not at peace with myself. Let me always seek to share Your Word with others, since this is what they need most of all. I humbly ask this in Christ's name, amen.

Beersheba—the Well of the Oath

BIBLE READING — GENESIS 21:22–34

LEARNING ABOUT FATHER ABRAHAM: Abimelech, the king of Gerar (the same king who previously wanted to marry the "single" Sarah), came with his chief captain, Phichol, to ask a favor of Abraham. He knew Abraham was a powerful man and a prophet of God, and that Abraham had God's blessing on him. Abimelech wanted to make a peace treaty with Abraham that would last through at least the next three generations. It is interesting to note that Abimelech, in speaking to Abraham, referred to God simply as "God" rather than "your God." This familiarity with God's name from this heathen king seems to indicate that he, too, had become a believer in the God of Abraham.

Abraham immediately agreed to Abimelech's request. However, Abraham informed Abimelech about a well of water Abimelech's servants had violently taken that Abraham had dug, and which was Abraham's by right. This incident was news to Abimelech. So what is the big deal over a well of water? Chiefly this: water is life for a herdsman and more valuable than gold.

To seal the peace treaty Abimelech asked for, Abraham gave Abimelech sheep and oxen, but he set apart seven female lambs. When Abimelech questioned him about them (being more valuable than male lambs since the female could reproduce), Abraham told Abimelech that he was giving him the lambs "from my hand" as his witness that Abraham had dug the well in question. Abraham called his well and the area surrounding it *Beersheba*, meaning "the well of the oath," signifying both the peace treaty with Abimelech and his declaration of ownership of that water source. Abimelech and Phichol left content with what had transpired.

Abraham planted trees near his well and, as was his custom, he communed with the LORD, his friend. He, Sarah, and Isaac, stayed for a long time in the land owned by the Philistines. Although God had promised this land to Abraham and his children, He had not yet given it to him.

THOUGHTS FROM MOTHER SARAH

As I watched my little Isaac play and grow, I knew I had to teach him all about our God. Here in the land of the Philistines, people religiously worshipped many gods. But my lord and I determined that our son would know all about the creator God, my lord's friend, the one who gave us this miracle child. Isaac would be the one to pass on his knowledge of God and of God's covenant with us to his future sons and daughters. I also wanted our son to become a godly man like his father. There were many distractions around us, so I had to protect Isaac and explain about right and wrong.

My beloved daughter, you have the grave responsibility to instruct your children. They are the next generation to know the God you love, worship, and serve, and we desire that they will become men and women of godly character. When God blessed you with children, He also gave you the responsibility of telling them about Him. If you don't teach your children why you fear and serve God and about all His goodness, both by your words and example, others will teach your children things they should not know.

BECOMING A FRIEND OF GOD

Despite Abraham's faults, shortcomings, and sins, he was a spiritual man whose heart was right with God. God got all the glory because of Abraham's words and actions. Spiritual leaders who sincerely love and serve God and teach others to do the same do so despite their faults and personality quirks.

Your local church is an apt place to get your feelings hurt, sometimes even by the pastor! Church leaders may rub you the wrong way or unintentionally slight or annoy you. If you have not been annoyed by a church leader, you probably have not gone to church long enough!

Suffering annoyances because of a church leader is not a reason to quit serving God, and it is certainly not a reason to quit attending church. Just as your spiritual leaders overlook your idiosyncrasies, your moodiness, and your behaviors, they also look to see the condition of your heart and your service to God. Therefore, you need to cut them some much-needed slack as they carry out the duties of their ministry. Look past their personalities and/or their odd manners and focus your attention on the God they serve.

Abraham was a straightforward communicator. So, too, God wants us to converse openly and honestly with each other. Communication is an act of love. Instead of assuming the worst about someone else's actions, it is best to kindly ask them about the motive behind their behavior.

Many times, the most common thing we Christian women do when we have a problem with someone is to talk to everyone else about our negative feelings instead of trying to talk with the offender directly to resolve the problem.

Very often, problems in marriages, friendships, families, work, and church are simply a result of indirect communication or not communicating at all. Instead of listening to rumors about someone, it is best to go directly to that person to clarify things.

When you hear about what someone else supposedly said or did, remember the example of Abraham before making any judgment on the person based on secondhand information. Broaching a difficult subject with someone else is not always easy to do, but it is respectful and honorable because it shows consideration of others and makes for peace and harmony in all kinds of relationships.

Words from Abraham's God

Proverbs 22:6 Train up a child in the way he should go: and when he is old, he will not depart from it.

Joel 1:3 Tell ye your children of it, and let your children tell their children, and their children another generation.

Romans 12:18 If it be possible, as much as lieth in you, live peaceably with all men.

Ephesians 4:32 Be ye kind one to another, tenderhearted, forgiving one another, even as God for Christ's sake hath forgiven you.

Hebrews 13:16 To do good and to communicate forget not: for with such sacrifices God is well pleased.

Prayer

Dear heavenly Father, in all my communications, both with my words and actions, help me to always point others to You. I ask that You help me in all my ways to glorify You in my life so that the good I do will reflect You.

Despite my sins and my failures, help me have my heart continually right before You so that others will see You in me and be attracted to Your righteousness. In this corrupt world, help me to make a difference while being a clear testimony of Your love, which You freely offer to all who will receive it. I sincerely ask this in the name of Christ Jesus. Amen.

God Tempted Abraham

BIBLE READING — GENESIS 22:1–10

LEARNING ABOUT FATHER ABRAHAM: Abraham was living in the land of the Philistines, specifically in Beersheba. Isaac was now a young man extremely loved by his parents. One day, God, the powerful creator, spoke to Abraham and told him to take Isaac to the land of Moriah and offer him as a burnt offering to Him. Abraham did not question this command; early the next morning he got up and took two of his servants, his son Isaac, and the necessary wood for the burnt offering and traveled to the place God directed him.

This journey took at least three days, and when Abraham was close to the specific spot, he told his servants to stay and wait while he and Isaac would journey on, have a private time of worship, and then come back. Abraham gave the wood for the fire to Isaac, and he carried the torch and the knife. When Isaac realized that something was missing for a burnt offering and asked the logical question, "Where is the lamb to be sacrificed?" Abraham wisely and tenderly replied, "God will provide himself a lamb."

This vague statement seemed to satisfy Isaac. The Bible doesn't say this, but possibly, at that point, Isaac may have realized that he was the intended sacrifice. When they got to the specific place God had chosen, Abraham built an altar, like he had done so many times before—he arranged the wood but then, instead of tying up a lamb, he tied up his precious and obedient son and placed him on the wood. Abraham then took the knife and held it high to make the killing of his beloved son as quick and as painless as possible.

In the narrative, what is so interesting is that Isaac never said a word or took any action to prevent himself from becoming a burnt offering—just like our Lord Jesus Christ did when His Father sent Him to die on the cross.

THOUGHTS FROM MOTHER SARAH

My lord told me that God had spoken to him, and I was eager to hear what God had said. But when Abraham revealed to me that God had told him to offer our special, beloved, only son as a burnt sacrifice, I was beyond horrified! Surely my lord had heard wrong! Our God was the God of life, not a god of death like all the gods that surrounded us. But my lord reminded me that we must love our God more than the gift He had given us. I couldn't accept it, but my lord was adamant. He was going to take our son and offer him to God like God had said, and there was nothing I could do to intervene. I knew in my heart that he was right; I just wished there would have been another way.

When Abraham and Isaac were away, I focused on all that I knew about God, all His promises to us, all of His provisions, and all the answered prayers.

My precious daughter, never allow your beloved children to come between you and God. While you love your children completely, you can easily make them an idol. Your family is a very wonderful gift from God, but always be careful to worship the giver of gifts rather than the gift itself.

BECOMING A FRIEND OF GOD

The ceremonial killing of children as part of the worship of various deities was a common practice among the people where Abraham lived. Now Abraham's God, his friend and creator, had told Abraham to sacrifice his son Isaac, and Abraham willingly obeyed. Clearly, Abraham had taught his son about God because Isaac offered no resistance when he realized he was to be the sacrificial "lamb" that was about to be put to death by his own father.

Abraham proved to God, Isaac, Sarah, and all who heard about his actions on that day that he loved his God more than he loved his son. Many years later, when Jesus was on earth, He said that to be His disciple (Luke 14:26) we must "hate" our family members. Loving and serving the family that God has given us is a service to God, but we need to love God so greatly that our love for our family pales in comparison. Abraham demonstrated this concept.

111

If we allow anyone or anything to come between us and God, that thing or person, even if it is our own child(ren), has become an idol. God, not our family, needs to be the object of our ultimate love. And like Abraham did, we need to demonstrate to our family that God does and will come first.

God deserves our perfect trust. Many times, His workings are mysterious and hard to understand; but He is our friend, and as such, He only wants the very best for us. Even when God does things that may grieve us deeply, He is working for our ultimate good.

Sometimes the greatest blessings that God has for us will be received in eternity. God is not only the God of this present life but also the God who will both receive us and bless us after our bodies are dead and our souls are alive in a new reality.

The place where Abraham went to sacrifice his son, a mountain in the land of Moriah, was the same place where Solomon, a great ancestor of Abraham, would build the first temple to worship Abraham's God. Then, many centuries later, after Solomon's temple would be destroyed on the same mount (believed by Bible scholars to be the New Testament Golgotha), another son of Abraham would be sacrificed, also by the will of His heavenly Father.

Words from Abraham's God

2 Chronicles 3:1 Solomon began to build the house of the LORD at Jerusalem in mount Moriah, where the LORD

appeared unto David his father, in the place that David had prepared in the threshing floor of Ornan the Jebusite.

Matthew 10:37 He that loveth father or mother more than me is not worthy of me: and he that loveth son or daughter more than me is not worthy of me.

Luke 14:26 If any man come to me, and hate not his father, and mother, and wife, and children, and brethren, and sisters, yea, and his own life also, he cannot be my disciple.

John 19:17 He bearing his cross went forth into a place called the place of a skull, which is called in the Hebrew Golgotha.

Hebrews 11:17–19 By faith Abraham, when he was tried, offered up Isaac: and he that had received the promises offered up his only begotten son, Of whom it was said, That in Isaac shall thy seed be called: Accounting that God was able to raise him up, even from the dead; from whence also he received him in a figure.

Prayer

Dear heavenly Father, I thank You that You are the God of life, not death, and that You tell us to choose life. But even as I do, help me to "put to death" any relationship, even if it is within my dear family, that comes between You and me. Help me love You in a way that is so much greater than the way I love them.

As I enjoy all that You have blessed me with, I want to worship You and You alone. Let my words and my actions proclaim my love and my trust in You, so that others will see You. I ask this in the name of Your precious Son, who You sent as a sacrifice for me. Amen.

DAY 22

Jehovah-Jireh

BIBLE READING — GENESIS 22:11–18

LEARNING ABOUT FATHER ABRAHAM: Just as Abraham was about to sacrifice Isaac, the angel of the LORD addressed Abraham with a message. Always sensitive to the words of God and ready to obey God's command, Abraham paused in the middle of his lethal, downward knife-thrust to answer the angel. The angel told him *not* to hurt his son, and he explained that the command to kill Isaac was only a test to see if Abraham was afraid to disobey God. The angel also told Abraham that he had passed this divine test with flying colors because he proved he would follow any command from God, even one to kill his son.

After both Abraham—and Isaac, no doubt—breathed a grateful sigh of relief, Abraham wanted to make a sacrifice of thanksgiving and praise to God. The altar was ready; all that was lacking was the appropriate animal. Abraham looked around and saw a ram caught in the bushy undergrowth behind him. This massive animal was held securely by his horns and was divinely placed there for Abraham's use. Abraham took the animal and joyfully offered it as a burnt offering to God in thankful worship. God had provided Abraham a ram for a sacrifice (not a lamb, as he had told Isaac earlier) and the ram was a suitable sacrificial animal to be offered as a substitute for Isaac.

To commemorate what God had done for them at this special place, Abraham named the place *Jehovah-jireh*, meaning "Jehovah will provide, and His provision will be made public."

God's angel then gave Abraham another message from God. This time, God confirmed His covenant with Abraham. God swore that He would bless Abraham and give him both physical and spiritual children. He added that these children would triumph over their enemies and that because of Abraham's obedience to God, all the nations of the world would be blessed. This future blessing was fulfilled when Jesus was born as a descendant of Abraham, and He gave His life to offer the gift of sinless, human, and eternal blood as the ultimate peace offering and salvation from hell to all the world.

THOUGHTS FROM MOTHER SARAH

When my lord and Isaac excitedly told me what had happened on the mountain, I was in joyful shock. I was so pleased with both of them! I felt ashamed of myself for ever doubting both my lord and our friend. I learned a powerful lesson and that is to fully trust our creator to do what is right by both of us.

My dear daughter, I hope you learn this lesson too, and even earlier in life than I did. Obeying God's commands, even when His instructions don't make any sense to you, will bring both calm peace and great blessing from Him. If you say, like we did,

that you love God, then you can trust Him by obeying His
commands—even when obedience is a fearful thing. Remember,
you will not see God's provision for you until He sees your
obedience to Him.

BECOMING A FRIEND OF GOD

It is vitally important as a Christian to obey God. It shows God
that we love Him. Jesus said, "If a man loves me, he will keep
my words" (John 14:23). Saying that we love God yet failing to
at least attempt to obey His Word shows that we really don't
love Him. Surrendering our will and our wishes to align with
His commands, despite what we want or what makes sense to
us, is an act of godly worship.

Obeying God is also an act of faith because obeying Him
means that we trust Him. When Abraham moved to sacrifice
his beloved son of promise, in direct obedience to God's
command, Abraham showed his total trust in God to take care
of them both. Obeying God may go against our ideas, our
understanding, or even common sense, but we do so by
trusting in God's goodness.

Our obedience to God is also a testimony to others. Jesus
instructed, "Let your light so shine before men, that they may
see your good works, and glorify your Father which is in
heaven" (Matthew 5:16). When we determine privately to obey
God, our public actions point others to our Savior, others who
might not see Him in action at any other time.

God blesses our obedience to Him, both in this life and in the
future, and the rewards for faithful obedience are beyond our

117

wildest imagination. Those rewards will far surpass any temporary trial or discomfort that we may encounter as we strive to obey.

Someday we will meet God face-to-face. Those who have obeyed God meet Him with joy; they have nothing to hide and they have done what they could. They showed their love for their Savior by doing what He asked them to do. But those who have disobeyed God's commands meet Him with shame. Obedience to God brings blessings, not regrets, while disobedience to God will bring long-term shame and regrets. If you truly want to be a closer friend of God, the key is to simply obey Him.

Words from Abraham's God

John 3:16 God so loved the world, that he gave his only begotten Son, that whosoever believeth in him should not perish, but have everlasting life.

Galatians 3:8–9 The scripture, foreseeing that God would justify the heathen through faith, preached before the gospel unto Abraham, saying, In thee shall all nations be blessed. So then they which be of faith are blessed with faithful Abraham.

Galatians 3:16 To Abraham and his seed were the promises made. He saith not, And to seeds, as of many; but as of one, And to thy seed, which is Christ.

Acts 3:25 Ye are the children of the prophets, and of the covenant which God made with our fathers, saying unto

Abraham, And in thy seed shall all the kindreds of the earth be blessed.

Hebrews 6:13-14 When God made promise to Abraham, because he could swear by no greater, he sware by himself, Saying, Surely blessing I will bless thee, and multiplying I will multiply thee.

Prayer

Dear heavenly Father, I am so grateful that I, too, can sincerely call You Jehovah-jireh, the God who provides. Thank You for Your daily provisions of peace in times of turmoil, answers to my prayers, strength for my day, and instruction from Your Holy Word.

Your greatest gift to me was the sacrifice of Your Son. Without His death, burial, and resurrection, all Your daily blessings to me would be both temporary and hollow.

Please help me to more fully obey Your commands given to me in Your Word. Help me live my life according to Your commandments so that others will see my obedience to You and give You glory and praise. I ask this in the name of Your precious Son, Jesus, who perfectly followed You and perfectly did Your will. Amen.

God Confirms His Covenant

BIBLE READING — GENESIS 22: 15–24

LEARNING ABOUT FATHER ABRAHAM: After these events transpired at Jehovah-jireh, Abraham and Isaac returned to the men waiting for them, and then they all returned home to Beersheba. While Abraham was mulling over the fantastic events he and Isaac had experienced on the mountain, and while thinking about God's latest messages to him, it's possible his mind may have gone back to the mysterious phrase "the seed of the woman." He knew that the word "seed" had a male connotation. It was a reproductive word always associated with men, not women; the fruit of the woman's womb was the result of the male seed.

Then he may have remembered his own words spoken to Isaac on that solemn trek up the mountain: "God will provide Himself a lamb." His mind may have gone to his miracle son, his seed, which he had placed in his ninety-year-old wife's dead womb. And then Abraham understood. God would somehow make Himself enter the womb of a woman who had not known a man. The woman's seed meant that the same God (who gave life to his wife's dead womb) would somehow be conceived in a virgin's untouched womb. Fathered by God Himself, this holy thing was to be a sacrificial, human lamb provided by God. It would be the ultimate sacrifice, the only sacrifice acceptable to a holy God.

Abraham finally saw God's plan clearly, and he rejoiced because he understood what God had meant—that one of his own physical descendants through Isaac would eventually bring forth this special woman whose womb God would borrow to birth this lamb.

Sometime later, Abraham got word that his brother Nahor and his wife Milcah had eight children, and that they had become grandparents because their son Bethuel had a daughter named Rebekah.

Thoughts from Mother Sarah

I was so overjoyed to see Isaac come home, and my lord too! While my lord told me about what had happened on the mountain, I could see what he was thinking. I remember this so clearly. He paused, and then he jumped up and exclaimed, "I see it now! I understand why I said, 'God will provide Himself a lamb.' He gave me a ram, but God will somehow make Himself to become a lamb—He will become the perfect, sinless human who will die. God will clothe Himself in flesh; He will be born as a human. God Himself, our friend, is the seed of the woman! He will come to be a sacrifice: a holy, perfect, human sacrifice for sinful humans like myself and all others. He must die or else He could not be a sacrifice. That is what He meant when He said that the serpent will bruise His heel but God will raise Him up! Because He is God, He will have power over death!"

After my lord explained all this to me, I, too, understood. At least, I think I did. It was deep yet wonderful and sad yet joyful. I could not help but think of His mother, who would, like me, give up her Son. I knew all the heart-wrenching, poignant, and distressing emotions she would feel. But I also knew that, like me, she would joyfully embrace her Son, her living, triumphant Son, like I did when Isaac returned.

Together, we humbly thanked our LORD, our friend, for revealing this to us, and we wondered why He had blessed us so greatly as to be in the lineage of this holy seed! We joyfully shared our discovery with Isaac, excited with the thought that one of his descendants would give birth to the promised seed, which had been promised so many years ago. Then we had to think about finding a suitable bride for our son, especially since I felt that my health was failing and I might not be alive much longer.

BECOMING A FRIEND OF GOD

God reveals His secrets to His friends. One blessing that God gives His friends is knowledge. Abraham, the friend of God was also a prophet, understood about the coming Savior. Daniel, known as a man "greatly beloved" (Daniel 9:23; 10:11, 19) was shown a snapshot of the world kingdoms that spanned future centuries. The apostle John, who God revealed the end times to (Revelation), was "the disciple whom Jesus loved" (John 13:23,19:26, 20:2).

Studying and meditating on God's Word will bring you more knowledge of the Word of God and of God Himself. God has revealed the future in the Bible because He gave the Bible as a love letter to His friends. Studying the Bible, both in a group setting or on your own, is where God will reveal His truth, and even His secrets, to you.

While Abraham had to wait for God to speak to him, we have God's Word revealed to us at our fingertips. The more we learn and study the Bible, the richer it becomes. The Bible is a living book, a physical manifestation of Jesus Christ, the Word made flesh (John 1:14). As you read and understand the Bible, you will find nuggets of truth that you can apply to your own life and circumstances. God's knowledge in the Scriptures is both a gift and a great blessing as you seek to establish a closer friendship with your God.

Words from Abraham's God

Matthew 1:23 Behold, a virgin shall be with child, and shall bring forth a son, and they shall call his name Emmanuel, which being interpreted is, God with us.

Luke 1:35 The angel answered and said unto her [Mary], The Holy Ghost shall come upon thee, and the power of the Highest shall overshadow thee: therefore also that holy thing which shall be born of thee shall be called the Son of God.

John 1:29 The next day John seeth Jesus coming unto him, and saith, Behold the Lamb of God, which taketh away the sin of the world.

John 8:56 Your father Abraham rejoiced to see my day: and he saw it, and was glad.

John 15:15 Henceforth I call you not servants; for the servant knoweth not what his lord doeth: but I have called you friends; for all things that I have heard of my Father I have made known unto you.

Prayer

Dear heavenly Father, help me understand and appreciate what a treasure I have in Your Word. So many times, I take my Bible for granted. I read it out of duty and obligation, often not fully comprehending Your personal message to me.

Remind me that as I read, You are speaking to me. Help me hear Your voice as I meditate on Your precious and holy words. Please give me a deeper understanding of this living and rich book, which is unlike any other book. I ask this in the name of Christ, amen.

DAY 24

The Death of Sarah

BIBLE READING — GENESIS CHAPTER 23

LEARNING ABOUT FATHER ABRAHAM: Abraham's beloved wife Sarah passed away at the age of 127 in the city of Kirjatharba. (Sarah had the honor of being the only woman in Scripture whose age is mentioned.) Abraham wept for her. After his initial shock and grief, he needed a place to properly bury her. While, no doubt, there had been other deaths and burials in Abraham's household prior to Sarah's, the loss of his beloved wife and companion moved Abraham to find a special burial place for her: a family burial plot. Since he didn't own any land himself, Abraham politely requested that the native inhabitants sell him a piece of land to bury Sarah on.

The children of Heth generously offered Abraham his choice of their sepulchers. With great politeness and humility, Abraham accepted, and he requested a particular piece of land that he desired—the cave of Machpelah, which was owned by

Ephron the Hittite. Ephron offered the land to Abraham as a gift, but Abraham politely refused and instead bought it for the appraised value of four hundred shekels of silver. The sale was a public, legal, and fair transaction, making Abraham the owner of the cave, the field, and all the trees on it. After the sale of the land was complete, Abraham buried Sarah. A graveyard that Abraham paid for in full was the first piece of land that Abraham owned out of all the vastness God had promised him.

THOUGHTS FROM MOTHER SARAH

Isaac was my source of joy and, of course, laughter. We had a very close bond. We talked often of his specialness, about how God fulfilled His promise to us and His plan for Isaac's future offspring. I knew I would not see these things in my lifetime, but I trusted God would allow me to see the fulfillment of His promises, even in a different plane of existence. One day I woke up feeling very weak. As the days went on, I grew weaker still. I knew that soon I would discard my earthly body. Abraham helped me as much as he could; he even asked a neighbor girl, Keturah, to be my nurse. She was wonderful.

One day my breathing became labored, my heart started racing, and I saw two men who I recognized as the same ones who came with our friend to tell me I would give birth to Isaac! They came this time to help me out of my uncomfortable, constricting, fleshly garment and to take me to a place called paradise. Now I could breathe freely, my senses were keener than ever, and my body was well, strong, and vibrant. My departed loved ones joyfully welcomed me. I finally feel totally fulfilled in this beautiful place. This is the home where I'd longed to be for so long!

BECOMING A FRIEND OF GOD

Our mourning and grief manifest our love for our precious loved ones who have passed away. It is normal and totally right to weep at a death or memory of a loved one. Jesus wept at the grave of His friend Lazarus (John 11:35), and His tears showed others His deep love for His friend. We grieve deeply because we love so intensely. But our mourning and tears, as severe as they may be, are tempered by knowing that, for the believer, our departed loved ones are both "absent from the body and present with the Lord" (2 Corinthians 5:8).

The apostle Paul told us that we are not to grieve as those who have no hope. It is right for us to be sorrowful at the death of our loved ones, but we have the promises of God that while unbelievers meet to part again, Christians part to meet again. If we believe Christ died and rose from the grave, God will bring those who sleep in Jesus with Him when He comes in the rapture for His own. Then all of us will be reunited with both Jesus and our loved ones, and we will be forever with the Lord (1 Thessalonians 4:13–14, 17).

The promise of heaven, given to all those who have accepted Christ as their Savior, is our comfort in our darkest grief. In our eternal home there will be no tears, no separation, no grief, and no mourning. This great assurance should not only comfort us when grieving; it should also motivate us to pray for and seek the salvation of those we love who have not yet

127

accepted Christ as their Savior and don't share the hope we have.

For the dying believer, death can be compared to going through a doorway. Those who can't breathe here can suddenly enjoy invigorating breaths; those with no strength become strong; those who are lonely will be reunited with loved ones; those who cannot play discard their physical bodies to join in happy games. Those of us left behind suffer devastating loss and endure great emotional pain, but as severe as our grief and mourning are, they are only temporary. Only time separates us from our dear ones who have accepted Christ as their Savior.

Words from Abraham's God

Isaiah 25:8 He will swallow up death in victory; and the Lord GOD will wipe away tears from off all faces; and the rebuke of his people shall he take away from off all the earth: for the LORD hath spoken it.

Matthew 5:4 Blessed are they that mourn: for they shall be comforted.

1 Corinthians 15:54 When this corruptible shall have put on incorruption, and this mortal shall have put on immortality, then shall be brought to pass the saying that is written, Death is swallowed up in victory.

2 Corinthians 5:4 We that are in this tabernacle do groan, being burdened: not for that we would be unclothed, but clothed upon, that mortality might be swallowed up of life.

1 Thessalonians 4:13 I would not have you to be ignorant, brethren, concerning them which are asleep, that ye sorrow not, even as others which have no hope.

Prayer

Dear heavenly Father, I hate death. Truly, it is an enemy. It seems that the older I get, the lonelier this life becomes, as one by one I say goodbye to loved ones, many whom I have known for nearly all of my life. But because of Your provision, I rejoice through my tears because their perfect lives have just begun, and it is only a matter of time before we are reunited forever.

Dear Father, give me a burden for those I love who don't have this promise. Help me to be burdened to pray for them, and give me wisdom to speak with them so that they, too, would ask You to save them like You did me, so that we can one day rejoice together in heaven. I ask this in the name of Your Son, Christ Jesus. Amen.

DAY 25

Abraham's Instructions to His Servant

BIBLE READING — GENESIS 24:1–9

LEARNING ABOUT FATHER ABRAHAM: At this point in Scripture, Abraham was an old man who had been extremely blessed by his friend the LORD. Now that his wife had passed away, he wanted to make sure that Isaac got married—but only to the right woman! And he had specific criteria for his future daughter-in-law. With that, Abraham entrusted the task of matchmaker to his oldest and most trusted servant. Before giving the servant specific details about the type of bride he had in mind, Abraham first had his servant put his hand under Abraham's thigh and swear by the LORD that he would follow his master's instructions explicitly.

While Abraham's instruction to his servant seems odd, British Methodist theologian and Bible scholar Adam Clarke (1762–1832), in his commentary on the Bible, offers a plausible and logical explanation for this seemingly strange request. Abraham wanted his servant to swear on the scar of God's covenant that was on his flesh, i.e., the scar of circumcision. We do something similar today when we ask someone to swear on a Bible.

Abraham made his servant swear that he would not take a shortcut and seek a local Canaanite woman for Isaac but instead make the long journey back to where Abraham's relatives lived and find a wife from among his relatives. Abraham was not being racist when he insisted on a non-Canaanite woman. This primary qualification was vital because Isaac's future wife needed to be a woman of faith in his God and not one who worshipped the false gods of the Canaanites.

The servant then asked a logical question: If the girl was not willing to leave her land, could he take Isaac to her? Abraham said no. Isaac was not to leave the land God had promised them. The girl was to come to them, to their land, and not the other way around.

Abraham reminded his servant that the LORD God who led him away from Ur of the Chaldees to the land of Canaan, the same God who had so richly blessed him in all things and given him great promises, would send His angel to guide the servant to the special woman God wanted to be Isaac's wife.

If the maiden would not follow the servant, she was not the right woman. In such a case, Abraham assured the servant that he would be clear from his oath. When the old, faithful servant put his hand under Abraham's thigh, he was not only solemnly promising his master but also God, Abraham's friend, that he would follow Abraham's instructions.

THOUGHTS FROM MOTHER SARAH

While I was still alive, my lord and I spoke often about a bride for Isaac. Isaac and I had a very close bond, and he was content to have me as the only woman in his life as long as I was alive. We taught Isaac all that we knew about the LORD God, especially about His promised seed of the woman who would eventually be one of his own descendants, and about how God, our friend, had chosen his father to be the beginning of a great nation.

I was so joyful that Isaac eagerly loved and worshipped God with us. We knew his bride had to understand and even love our God like we did. She had to be a woman of our faith, not a woman who worshipped the false gods throughout this land.

My precious daughter, what I desired for my firstborn son is what I desire also for you. Although we are separated by thousands of years, it is just as important now for you to have a husband who is a God-fearing man as it was for me then. If you do, thank God for him. If you don't, pray for him that God would speak to his heart. In the meantime, love him, praise him, submit to his leadership, and strive that your spiritual walk and the whole of your life will be an example for him.

BECOMING A FRIEND OF GOD

While arranged marriages, such as the one Abraham fashioned for Isaac, are not commonplace in American culture, the principle of marrying a person of similar faith is still vitally important for a happy relationship. A godly woman wants to please God; and out of trust in and obedience to God, she will kindly and lovingly submit to the leadership of her husband. A Christian man who loves God will show love to his wife.

Any marriage relationship is hard because it involves two sinful, imperfect people who are expected to get along with each other. Marital disaster can occur quickly when one partner desires to love and please God and glorify Him through his life, while the other does not.

Marriage is a partnership: two people working toward a single goal but often in different ways. The broad goal for every Christian marriage is for both individuals to serve and glorify God while supporting and encouraging each other. Marriage can be wonderful or it can be a disaster. When a child of God yokes himself with a child of the devil, they will have problems with their father-in-law. An unequal marriage yoke causes stress and unhappiness for both partners and strife in the home, and it limits how the believing spouse can effectively serve God. This type of miserable relationship may prematurely end in divorce.

Many times, a Christian woman will fall in love with an unsaved man, erroneously thinking that after the marriage vows, he will change for the better. This rarely occurs. God gave the command to believers to not yoke themselves with an unbeliever because He wants Christians to enjoy each other in the institution of marriage. A happy, harmonious, mutually fulfilling, and loving marriage is a gift from God, and such a relationship brings Him glory.

Words from Abraham's God

Deuteronomy 7:3-4 Neither shalt thou make marriages with them; thy daughter thou shalt not give unto his son, nor his daughter shalt thou take unto thy son. For they will turn away thy son from following me, that they may serve other gods: so will the anger of the LORD be kindled against you, and destroy thee suddenly.

Amos 3:3 Can two walk together, except they be agreed?

Proverbs 19:14 House and riches are the inheritance of fathers: and a prudent wife is from the LORD.

2 Corinthians 6:14 Be ye not unequally yoked together with unbelievers: for what fellowship hath righteousness with unrighteousness? and what communion hath light with darkness?

Ephesians 5:23 The husband is the head of the wife, even as Christ is the head of the church: and he is the savior of the body.

Prayer

Dear heavenly Father, thank You for creating the institution of marriage. Thank You especially for my husband. Instruct me as to how I can please my husband and encourage him to love You more. I know that as he loves and serves You, he will also desire to please me. Please strengthen and protect our marriage and direct us so that we can together serve and glorify both You and each other. Help us to strive for peace and happiness in our home. I ask this in Jesus's name, amen.

DAY 26

The Servant Meets Rebekah

BIBLE READING — GENESIS 24:10–28

LEARNING ABOUT FATHER ABRAHAM: The servant Abraham entrusted to find the proper wife for his son also had the responsibility of managing all of Abraham's goods. So he took ten of Abraham's camels, along with needed supplies and other servants who were, more than likely, armed for the long journey, and traveled to Mesopotamia—the city where Abraham's brother Nahor lived. The servant arrived at the city's well in the evening when the women of the city came to get water for their homes.

The next step was to find the right woman. The servant prayed to Abraham's God and asked Him for a specific sign. He told God that he was going to ask a young woman for a drink of water, and if she was the right woman to be Isaac's bride, then she would also offer to water his ten camels.

Before he was finished praying, Rebekah, the granddaughter of Abraham's brother, came to the well with her pitcher. The servant noticed that she was an exquisite girl, and the Bible also records that she was a virgin. After Rebekah filled her pitcher with water, the servant approached her and asked for a drink. She immediately obliged, and when he finished drinking, she offered to water all ten of his thirsty camels too! While she was watering the camels, the servant watched her and wondered if God had truly answered his prayers and if this was the right girl for Isaac.

When all the camels had finished drinking, the servant gave Rebekah a golden earring and two golden bracelets as a gift for her kindness and help. Then he asked her who she was and if he could lodge with her family for the night. She told him she was Bethuel's daughter, Abraham's great niece, and she assured the servant that he and his camels were welcome to spend the night with them.

Before the servant accepted her invitation of hospitality, he humbly bowed his head and worshipped the LORD. In his prayer, the servant praised God for His goodness toward his master, Abraham, realizing that God had led him to this woman and the family of Abraham's brother. Meanwhile, Rebekah ran back to her mother's house to tell her what had happened and to let her know that they would have a guest for the night.

THOUGHTS FROM MOTHER SARAH

I had known Nahor all my life, and Milcah was a wonderful wife to him. They were good people and, like myself and Abraham, they did not worship the gods of the surrounding peoples. They, too, worshipped our LORD, the one creator God, and taught their family to worship Him also. A granddaughter of Nahor and Milcah would be an excellent choice of a wife for my son, Isaac. My dear daughter, while I never had a physical daughter, I hope that you have traits like Rebekah too. She knew and worshipped our God and she was friendly, kind, helpful, hardworking, and sexually pure. These are virtues that make any woman both desirable and beautiful.

BECOMING A FRIEND OF GOD

Abraham's servant prayed a very specific prayer and got exactly what he asked for.

There are benefits to specific prayers. In Mark 10:46–52, blind Bartimaeus called out to Jesus to have mercy on him. This was a very general request. Then Jesus asked him what he wanted—specifically—and he answered that he wanted his sight. Jesus knew exactly what Bartimaeus wanted because He was God, but He wanted Bartimaeus to verbalize his specific request. Then, after he asked, Jesus gave him his sight. James 4:2 tells us that "ye have not, because ye ask not." This verse has the lesson of asking for specific wants and needs. Had Bartimaeus not asked for his sight, Jesus may not have given it to him.

While it is fine to pray general prayers such as, "Help me, God!" and it is honorable and shows our personal trust in our heavenly Father, when we communicate the specific desires of our heart to Him, it is even better.

God invites us to petition Him with purpose. In Isaiah 45:11, He says, "Ask me of things to come concerning my sons, and concerning the work of my hands command ye me." Specific prayers arise from an uncluttered mind. These are serious and focused prayers, not flippant. As we see God work in precise ways to answer our prayers, we grow stronger in faith.

Asking God for specific things creates a lighter load for us to bear. When we have a particular burden that we have identified in our mind, and then we purposely move it from us to God in prayer, we can remember throughout the day that we have given God our burden. This is just as He told us to do (1 Peter 5:7), and we can rest in knowing our burden is no longer ours; it is His problem, and He can deal with it as He sees fit.

Abraham's servant also teaches us another lesson. He "put feet to his prayers" after he asked God for precisely what he wanted, and we need to do the same. By faith we need to walk toward what we have asked for, trusting that God has gone before us to prepare His perfect answers to our personal requests.

Words from Abraham's God

Psalm 37:5 Commit thy way unto the LORD; trust also in him; and he shall bring it to pass.

Proverbs 16:3 Commit thy works unto the LORD, and thy thoughts shall be established.

Jeremiah 29:12 Then shall ye call upon me, and ye shall go and pray unto me, and I will hearken unto you.

Jeremiah 33:3 Call unto me, and I will answer thee, and shew thee great and mighty things, which thou knowest not.

1 Peter 5:7 Casting all your care upon him; for he careth for you.

Prayer

Dear heavenly Father, I know You know all things, yet You have given me a mind to think and to reason. I thank You that You are never tired of hearing from me. Help me to not tire of hearing from You. Thank You that You are a God of detail, and that there is nothing too small for me to bring to Your kind attention.

Help me to pray with purpose and to be serious about my prayers, talking to You as my friend and my helper. Keep me mindful to consult with You about all my decisions. As You give me answers to my prayers, let me be careful to thank You and give You the glory. In Christ's name I ask this, amen.

Rebekah's Family

BIBLE READING — GENESIS 24:29–61

LEARNING ABOUT FATHER ABRAHAM: After Rebekah went home to tell her mother about Abraham's servant, whom she had met at the well, her brother Laban invited him to stay with them, informing him that they had prepared a place for him and for his camels; but the faithful man refused to eat until he told them about his purpose for having come.

The man introduced himself as the servant of Abraham, their blood relative, and he briefly summarized the life of his master. The servant first mentioned Abraham's wealth, giving credit to the LORD. Then he told them about Sarah giving birth to Isaac when she was old and quickly followed that by saying that Isaac was the heir to all Abraham owned. He then related that Isaac needed a wife who worshiped God from among his relatives and not a Canaanite woman, and that the angel of the LORD had guided and directed him to them.

Abraham's servant then told his master's family members what had happened at the well: how Rebekah had done exactly what he had asked of the LORD.

After hearing this fantastic account, both Laban and Bethuel, Rebekah's brother and father, told the servant that Rebekah could go back with him to be Isaac's wife. After receiving this permission from the men concerning their sister and daughter, the servant again humbly worshipped the LORD. Then he brought out precious gifts of jewels and clothing for Rebekah and her family. After they accomplished the business at hand, the servant and his men ate, drank, and rested for the night.

The next morning, the servant was ready to start the journey back home with Rebekah, but Rebekah's mother and brother wanted him to stay a few days longer, at least ten, perhaps to get used to the idea that they would likely never see Rebekah again. Abraham's servant was adamant; he wanted to leave with her immediately. Rebekah's family asked Rebekah if she would go with the man, and she agreed. Her family gave her a parting prophetic blessing, telling her to be the mother of "thousands of millions" and declaring her offspring would be victorious over their enemies.

Then the servant started back home with Rebekah and her nurse. His mission had been successful.

THOUGHTS FROM MOTHER SARAH

Rebekah is a woman of great faith. It must have been hard for her to leave the only family she knew and step out into the unknown. But she knew, based on the gifts that our servant brought her, that if she became the wife of his master's son, she would have so much more. What she would leave behind was so little compared to what lay ahead of her in her new life.

BECOMING A FRIEND OF GOD

Like Rebekah we, too, have a choice to make. After we have accepted Christ as our Savior, He offers us an opportunity to serve Him. Service to God can be difficult. He does not guarantee that those who serve Him will have endless health and wealth, nor does He promise them life without hardships. Just read about the apostle Paul in the book of Acts! But God does not ask anyone to give of themselves or of their resources without rewarding them.

You cannot outgive God. He gives His faithful servants gifts of peace, joy, direction, and help in various ways. These blessings and gifts from God are both priceless yet small when compared to the wonderful rewards that await faithful servants in heaven. Our mind cannot comprehend all the beauty and the glories of eternity that God has in store for our faithful service in this life.

God does not make or force anyone to serve Him; but He sees the efforts of those who desire to give back to Him, tell others about Him, and support His work, and He richly rewards them with His blessings.

Just as Rebekah saw the benefit of becoming Isaac's wife, partly because of the gifts brought by the servant, so, too, may all of us realize the benefits of living our life in service for God.

Words from Abraham's God

1 Samuel 12:24 Only fear the LORD, and serve him in truth with all your heart: for consider how great things he hath done for you.

Psalm 16:11 Thou wilt shew me the path of life: in thy presence is fulness of joy; at thy right hand there are pleasures for evermore.

Malachi 3:16–17 They that feared the LORD spake often one to another: and the LORD hearkened, and heard it, and a book of remembrance was written before him for them that feared the LORD, and that thought upon his name. And they shall be mine, saith the LORD of hosts, in that day when I make up my jewels; and I will spare them, as a man spareth his own son that serveth him.

John 12:26 If any man serve me, let him follow me; and where I am, there shall also my servant be: if any man serve me, him will my Father honor.

Colossians 3:24 Knowing that of the Lord ye shall receive the reward of the inheritance: for ye serve the Lord Christ.

Prayer

Dear heavenly Father, You have done so much for me, far more than I can ever imagine. It is an honor to serve You, the most powerful being in the universe. Thank You for the opportunity to be of service to You. You are far beyond what my mind can conceive, yet I know I am special to You and that I am part of something very great because of You.

Let me see, with eyes of faith, a glimpse of the wonders You have for all those who serve You. Help me to invest this life in eternal blessings that are far beyond my imagination. Help me to be faithful so that when I finally meet You face-to-face, I will hear Your words of praise to me: "Well done, thou good and faithful servant; … enter thou into the joy of thy Lord." In Jesus's name, I pray, amen.

Isaac and Rebekah

BIBLE READING — GENESIS 24: 58–67

LEARNING ABOUT FATHER ABRAHAM: Rebekah answered her family's question about leaving with the beautiful words, "I will go." Rebekah then departed from her family, her city, and all that she knew—apart from taking some of her maidservants with her—with Abraham's servant and his men to meet and marry a man she had never seen before.

The caravan of camels left on their long return journey to the land of Canaan. A few hours before the caravan arrived, Isaac went out to the field to meditate. While we are not told what he was thinking about while he was waiting for his father's servant to return, Isaac might have been thinking of Abraham's words concerning their God, specifically in relation to the servant's task of finding his bride. Picture Isaac standing in the grass, seeing the camels coming, and seeing Rebekah get her first glimpse of her future husband.

Out of respect for Isaac, her superior, who was on foot, Rebekah did not remain seated on her mount but politely dismounted. To show both modesty and subjection to her intended husband, she covered herself with a veil.

Abraham's servant joyfully gave Isaac a detailed account of all that had transpired, proving that God had indeed guided him and chosen Rebekah as his wife. After the marriage ceremony and festivities, Isaac took Rebekah to his deceased mother Sarah's tent, and the place of mourning and death became a place of rejoicing as the two became one flesh.

Despite this being an arranged marriage, Isaac fell in love with his new wife. The sweetness of being married to the kind and lovely Rebekah was just what Isaac needed to help heal the grief of his mother's death.

THOUGHTS OF MOTHER SARAH

I was thrilled when my son finally met his promised bride! And then they honored me by enjoying their honeymoon and beginning of married life in my former tent! Isaac needed the comfort that only a wife could bring him, since he was still missing me. My daughter, among the many things that you are to your husband, you are a comfort to him. Let the kind actions of my daughter-in-law be a reminder of that to you in your own marriage.

BECOMING A FRIEND OF GOD

Meditation is the act of intentionally focusing your mind on something. All humans meditate. Many times, our meditations are comprised of thoughts on our relationships, family issues, workplace woes, finances, current world events, or the latest posts on social media. However, it is a command of God that His people should meditate on His Word and His works.

The words "meditate" and "meditation" are used twenty times in the King James Version of the Bible. While meditation can lead us to praise, prayer, and worship of God, it is a separate act and an active process—a type of exercise to train one's mind. Our mind is a muscle, and we need to train it to work for us, just as we physically train our bodies to do everything else. To have a time of focused thought on God's Word and His goodness is to exercise our mind "muscle" so that the truths of God's power, His love, His promises, and His instructions are mentally brought to us in our present and sometimes difficult circumstances.

One way to meditate on God's goodness is to keep a written journal of it. Writing the date and the specific answer that God gave you to a particular request is helpful to remember the things that God has done for you. As you meditate on God's past blessings and past answers to your prayers, your faith will grow, and you'll be encouraged by how God will help you with both present and future difficulties.

Meditation can also be a part of your daily prayer time as you think about exactly what you want to say to God. Despite the fact that God is truly a mind reader, focusing your thoughts is a type of meditation. Meditation should be a part of reading the Bible. You have the words in front of you, provided and preserved by God for your personal use. As you read the Bible, do so slowly and thoughtfully, mentally "chewing" the verses in your mind and looking for truths that perhaps escaped you in prior readings. Thinking about God's Word as you read it is a way of storing it in your mind for future use.

If you don't take the time and mental energy to focus on God's Word, then you will have nothing for the Holy Spirit to bring to your remembrance when you need it, either for your own comfort and encouragement or to help others. It is your responsibility to meditate on God's Word, and it is His joy to give His words back to you when you need them the most. Take some time every day for some godly mediation.

Words from Abraham's God

Genesis 2:24 Therefore shall a man leave his father and his mother, and shall cleave unto his wife: and they shall be one flesh.

Joshua 1:8 This book of the law shall not depart out of thy mouth; but thou shalt meditate therein day and night, that thou mayest observe to do according to all that is written therein: for then thou shalt make thy way prosperous, and then thou shalt have good success.

Psalm 19:14 Let the words of my mouth, and the meditation of my heart, be acceptable in thy sight, O LORD, my strength, and my redeemer.

Song of Solomon 4:9 Thou hast ravished my heart, my sister, my spouse; thou hast ravished my heart with one of thine eyes, with one chain of thy neck.

Ephesians 5:25 Husbands, love your wives, even as Christ also loved the church, and gave himself for it.

Prayer

Dear heavenly Father, help me to be kind and respectful to my husband. Help me treat him every day as I would an honored friend, and help me give of myself to him as he needs me. As I show him my love, increase our love for each other and also help us both love You more.

Help me make meditating on Your Word a daily habit, and reward me with the treasures that are found in Your Word. Please help me replace some of my useless meditation with frequent thoughts of You and Your Word, and help me remember and thank You for Your daily blessings and frequent answers to my prayers. I ask these things in the name of Christ Jesus, amen.

Abraham and Keturah

BIBLE READING — GENESIS 25:1–6

LEARNING ABOUT FATHER ABRAHAM: After Isaac was happily married, Abraham married again when he was about one hundred and forty years old. His new wife's name was Keturah, which means "incense." As his age wasn't any consideration, he had six sons with her: Zimran, Jokshan, Medan, Midian, Ishbak, and Shuah. These six sons of Abraham eventually became the heads of several present-day Arab nations. The most notable son was Midian, whose descendants produced Jethro, the father-in-law of Moses, several hundred years later.

Abraham began to prepare for his death. While he was still alive, Abraham gave all that he had to Isaac, but he first gave rich gifts of both livestock and wealth to Keturah's sons and Ishmael. Then Abraham sent away Keturah's sons, and possibly even Keturah herself. Abraham directed them eastward to the area of what is the modern-day Arabian Peninsula and the country of Jordan. With the parting gifts of their inheritance, and his direction, Abraham knew that Keturah's sons could carve out a life for themselves and settle in a country far from the land God had promised to give him and Isaac.

This prudent decision ensured there would be no future disputes or conflicts between the sons of Isaac and the sons of Keturah over the promised land. Abraham knew that all his sons would become heads of great nations, but the land that God promised Abraham was meant exclusively for Isaac and his offspring.

THOUGHTS FROM MOTHER SARAH

I was glad that my lord Abraham remarried. Before I died, I had given him my blessing to find another wife. Keturah took excellent care of me when I was sick and dying, and I knew she would be very good to my lord as well. It thrilled me to know that he would be a father again. My job was to conceive and raise Isaac, and I accomplished my mission, but God still had work for my lord before he would join me.

BECOMING A FRIEND OF GOD

Age is no barrier to service for our Lord. While our ability to serve God may change with advancing years, God has a job for all of His servants. He has promised that "every man shall receive his own reward *according to his own labor*" (1 Corinthians 3:8). So when physical, or even mental, infirmities make our service for God more difficult, then rejoice, because your heavenly rewards increase!

A side benefit of serving God, especially in old age, is that it continues to give the elderly purpose for their lives. As they look beyond themselves to the needs of others, their work for God also becomes an excellent way to combat the depression that is often associated with loneliness.

A great example of serving God in advanced years is my mother. When she was in her eighties, she was very active in her church, reaching out to both young and old ladies, teaching Sunday school, playing the piano, and entertaining in her home. She was faithful to attend all church services, including weekly door-to-door visitation. When her health rapidly declined and she had to rely more on public transportation, she would witness to the van driver. When he told her he did not talk about either religion or politics, she said that was fine, she would do the talking! And she did. The very day that she was taken to heaven, a few months after her ninetieth birthday, my mother was weak and on her deathbed, yet she was witnessing to her unsaved cousin, telling him she wanted him to go to heaven—where she would be—when he died. My mother knew that age was not a barrier to serving the Lord, and so she served Him faithfully until her life on earth was finished.

No matter how old you are, now is the time to make serving God both a habit and a priority. Make it a point to do something every day in service for the Lord. If nothing else, make a prayer list and pray for Christian workers for wisdom, for people you know to get saved, and for government leaders for salvation, wisdom, and direction in their daily tasks.

Prayer is a task that any Christian can, and should, be actively doing. Never believe that the "only thing" you can do is pray. Petitioning the God of the universe for favor and help is both a fantastic work and a great privilege. Not everyone in the world can do this.

There is no retirement age in the service of the Lord, but God has promised His servants a rest. That rest will come, but not until we are with Him, enjoying His presence and the wonderful rewards He has promised us.

Words from Abraham's God

Psalm 92:14 They shall still bring forth fruit in old age; they shall be fat and flourishing.

Proverbs 16:31 The hoary head is a crown of glory, if it be found in the way of righteousness.

Luke 19:13 And he called his ten servants, and … said unto them, Occupy till I come.

1 Corinthians 15:58 Therefore, my beloved brethren, be ye stedfast, unmoveable, always abounding in the work of the Lord, forasmuch as ye know that your labor is not in vain in the Lord.

Hebrews 6:10 God is not unrighteous to forget your work and labor of love, which ye have shewed toward his name, in that ye have ministered to the saints, and do minister.

Prayer

Dear heavenly Father, thank You for the life and the years You have blessed me with already. As the years go on, I ask that You continue to give me strength for all my days. Help me realize that every day of life is a precious gift from You.

Help me to not become lazy or complacent as I grow older, and as my time gets nearer to meeting You, help me to be mindful of meeting You and to seek to serve You more, and better, so that I will truly finish my days well. Help me to daily invest my earthly years into heavenly retirement rewards as I serve You in whatever capacity You provide. I ask this in the name of Christ, amen.

DAY 30

The Death of Abraham

BIBLE READING — GENESIS 25:7–10

LEARNING ABOUT FATHER ABRAHAM: After Abraham lived to be 175 years old, his physical body died and the angels carried his soul to paradise (Luke 16:22). There, Sarah and others who had gone on before him joyfully greeted him. Paradise was the waiting area for the souls of departed Old Testament saints because they could not yet be received directly into heaven—the way to God's abode was not yet opened. Entrance into the actual presence of God had to wait many years until Jesus (the most notable son of Abraham) gave His sinless, human, and everlasting blood as an atonement for sin. He was the promised seed of the woman, and being both man and God, His death allowed God the Father to open the way to heaven. In the meantime, at the gate of paradise, Abraham welcomed all his children to this perfect place of eternal peace and everlasting family reunion.

Meanwhile, back on earth, Abraham's first two sons, Ishmael and Isaac, buried their father next to Sarah in the cave of Machpelah—the family plot.

Ishmael returned from his country to visit his father before his death, perhaps after Abraham sent Keturah's sons away. He might have realized that his father's death was not long in coming and wanting to care for him and attend his funeral. Isaac and Ishmael mourned together over the body of the great man who gave life to both of them.

The field containing the burial plot for Abraham and Sarah would later also receive Isaac and Rebekah and their grandson Jacob and his wife Leah over the years.

THOUGHTS FROM MOTHER SARAH

It seemed that I had just been received into paradise myself when my precious lord, the love of my life, Abraham, joined me. I wasn't even finished greeting him before Isaac and my daughter-in-law Rebekah were here too! While decades had passed in the world that I left, I didn't even have time to consider the loved ones I left behind before they, too, were with me here in this wonderful place.

Here in paradise, my lord is the first to greet and welcome all our children. He reaches up to joyfully grab each precious child, and he holds them close to his bosom! All our children immediately recognize us when they come here, even though they were born long after we died. When Abraham releases them, I am the next to hug and welcome them to this place of everlasting joy where we are finally all together.

BECOMING A FRIEND OF GOD

Although Abraham's life was not free of fleshly, carnal struggles, his faith—and at times lack of it—caused him to love, trust, and cultivate a friendship with God. When Abraham's physical body died, his soul, the real Abraham, became free. He was changed into a fully spiritual being, one that was more like his God. His friendship with God continued but in a spiritual, deeper, and far closer way now that Abraham could interact face-to-face with Him.

Abraham never stopped existing. He left this world behind, like a bad dream, and woke up changed and in a place of existence that was far more real to him than his life on earth. The same will be for all of us who have accepted Jesus Christ as our Savior and who are spiritual children of Abraham.

We, too, will leave this present world, be changed, and become more fully alive than we have ever been before. We will be changed to be like our Savior, and we will meet Christ face-to-face to be welcomed into fulness of life for eternity.

Heaven is a wonderful place, and what makes it so desirable is simply the presence of God. Do not be fooled by what the world tells you—heaven without the presence of God is not heaven. God's goodness will fill and permeate all aspects of heaven. In heaven, all personality conflicts will disappear, and there will be no doctrinal differences among Christians. As God is good, so we, too, will be filled with His goodness, so much so that the fulness of His thoughts, His peace, His joy, His laughter, and His smiles will pour out of us.41555

If you intend to go to heaven and to be with God for eternity, now is the time to cultivate your friendship with the God of heaven. Then, when you stand before Him, He will welcome you to His everlasting abode as His dear, precious child.

Having a personal relationship with Jesus Christ, God's only begotten Son, will guarantee that He will not say to you as He will say to many, "Depart from me, ye cursed, into everlasting fire, prepared for the devil and his angels" (Matthew 25:41). Start today to bring a bit of heaven into your heart and life by deepening your personal relationship with God, the source of all heavenly delights.

Words from Abraham's God

Psalm 16:11 Thou wilt shew me the path of life: in thy presence is fulness of joy; at thy right hand there are pleasures for evermore.

Matthew 6:20–21 Lay up for yourselves treasures in heaven, where neither moth nor rust doth corrupt, and where thieves do not break through nor steal: For where your treasure is, there will your heart be also.

Luke 16:22 It came to pass, that the beggar died, and was carried by the angels into Abraham's bosom.

John 14:2 In my Father's house are many mansions: if it were not so, I would have told you. I go to prepare a place for you.

1 Corinthians 2:9 As it is written, Eye hath not seen, nor ear heard, neither have entered into the heart of man, the things which God hath prepared for them that love him.

Prayer

Dear heavenly Father, help me to not only strive to deepen my communication with You but also to encourage others to enter a personal relationship with You. To have a friend like You is to have a friend who sticks closer than a brother. There is no relationship on earth that can compare to a friendship with You, and I am both humbled and thrilled that You, who are so far above me in all Your ways, want to be my friend.

Help me strive to get to know You better in this body of flesh and to look eagerly forward to being changed, having a glorified body like You, and finally meeting You face-to-face. Seeing You in person and in Spirit will be the best experience of my life. I will then get to be with You and fully enjoy all Your blessings for eternity. I humbly thank You and praise You for Your great goodness, and it is all because of Your Son, Christ Jesus. Amen.

Epilogue

PAST, PRESENT, AND FUTURE

If you think Abraham is dead and gone, you are only partly right. Abraham's body is dead and buried, but Abraham is still very much alive. Many years after Abraham's death, when God talked with Moses (one of Abraham's descendants), He told Moses, "I am the God of Abraham" (Exodus 3:6). Then, centuries later, Jesus referred to this incident (Matthew 22:32), and He added an interesting observation, saying, "God is not the God of the dead, but of the living," confirming that Abraham, although gone from this present world, is still alive.

Prophetically speaking, Abraham must be alive because God still "owes" Abraham some things, and He will make sure that Abraham gets everything that has been promised.

God promised that He would make Abraham into a great nation (Genesis 12:1). The nation of Israel traces its roots back to its father Abraham.

God promised that Abraham's "seed," his offspring, would be as numerous as the dust of the earth (Genesis 13:16; 22:17). Abraham is not only the father of the Jewish nation but also, through his sons with Hagar and Keturah, the father of many of the Arab nations. This fulfilled the promise of God when He said that Abraham would be the father of "many nations" (Genesis 17:4–5). All the Jewish and Arab people who have been born, lived, and died throughout the centuries are truly as many as dust particles and sand grains.

God promised that He would make Abraham's seed as numerous as "the stars of heaven" (Genesis 15:5, 22:17). This is referring to spiritual offspring. All those people throughout the centuries who accepted Abraham's God as their Savior and friend are also Abraham's seed. This great number is as great as the multitude of the stars of heaven.

God promised Abraham vast land ownership several times (Genesis 12:7; 13:15; 15:7, 18; 17:8). But when Abraham died, the only piece of land he owned was a burial plot! Again, God still "owes" him much more land than that, and He will make sure that both Abraham and his children get it. Jesus referred to this future event when He said, "Many shall come from the east and west, and shall sit down with Abraham, and Isaac, and Jacob, in the kingdom of heaven" (Matthew 8:11). In a future time, which Jesus referred to as "the kingdom of heaven," Abraham and his children will possess and enjoy the land God promised to him centuries ago. The Jews have their own land, the country of Israel, but it is only a piece of the land that God promised to Abraham, specifically "from the river of Egypt unto the great river, the river Euphrates" (Genesis 15:18). Presently, the nation of Israel is within this area, but Israel's present borders are not as vast as those God promised to Abraham. Eventually, in the future kingdom of heaven, the Jews will possess all the land God promised to them.

God promised to make Abraham's name great (Genesis 12:2). Abraham was a great man, and he was referred to as "a mighty prince" (Genesis 23:6) by the Canaanites. While that was a significant distinction, Abraham's fame continued and was vastly expanded after his death. Today, members of the three major monotheistic religions of the world—Judaism, Christianity, and Islam—recognize Abraham as a great man.

God promised He would bring "a gift" through Abraham and that all the families and nations of the earth would be blessed (Genesis 12:3; 18:18; 22:18). This mysterious blessing that came through Abraham was nothing less than the person of the Lord Jesus Christ. Because God so greatly loved all the families and nations of the world, He gave them the gift of His Son (John 3:16). Because of Jesus's sacrifice, all the nations of the world can have the gift of everlasting life in heaven with God, Abraham, and all of his spiritual children.

While all the promises to Abraham are very interesting, we can benefit from the blessings of God to Abraham too. God told Abraham, "I will bless them that bless thee, and curse him that curseth thee" (Genesis 12:3). This promise is just as pertinent to us today as it was to Abraham in his day. Centuries later, David, another of Abraham's descendants, reminded us of this when he wrote the command of God and its rewards in Psalm 122.

"Pray for the peace of Jerusalem: they shall prosper that love thee" (Psalm 122:6).

163

Dear Friend

Dear friend, thank you for reading my book. It is a great honor to me that you have chosen to read what I have written. But before you go, I want to ask you a very personal question: Are you absolutely sure that when you die you are bound for heaven?

Many women call themselves "Christian" because they believe in God, Jesus, and even the Holy Spirit, and this is all very good. They may pray to Jesus too. But Jesus addressed this when He said,

> Not every one that saith unto me, Lord, Lord, shall enter into the kingdom of heaven; but he that doeth the will of my Father which is in heaven. Many will say to me in that day, Lord, Lord, have we not prophesied in thy name? and in thy name have cast out devils? and in thy name done many wonderful works? And then will I profess unto them, I never knew you: depart from me, ye that work iniquity.
>
> —Matthew 7:21–23

Wow! These are very powerful and harsh words! Jesus is saying He will personally tell some people to depart from Him, to actually go into hell, even though while they were alive, they prophesied in His name, cast out devils, and did many wonderful works. What they did may be more than what you've ever done or will ever do.

My desire, and even more importantly God's desire, for you is that you know for sure that when you do meet Jesus face-to-face, He will welcome you into His holy heaven forever instead of saying, "Depart from me, ye that work iniquity." If you have any doubts about this, I pray you would make sure of this now.

The Bible, God's Holy Word to mankind, records, "These things have I written unto you that believe on the name of the Son of God; that ye may know that ye have eternal life, and that ye may believe on the name of the Son of God" (1 John 5:13). You can know *now* that you are assured of Jesus welcoming you into heaven when you die. Jesus said, "Ye must be born again" (John 3:7). Since He has made being born again a requirement for both salvation and heaven, He also tells you how to become born again.

You must first realize that you are a sinner and that your sins have separated you from God. "All have sinned, and come short of the glory of God" (Romans 3:23). As a sinner, you are condemned to death. "The wages of sin is death" (Romans 6:23). We have all earned those wages! This death is not only a physical death but even more seriously, spiritual death, which is eternal separation from God in hell. "It is appointed unto men once to die, but after this the judgment"

(Hebrews 9:27). After you physically die, you will still be spiritually alive to be judged by God to see if He deems you worthy to enter His heaven.

The certain news is that you cannot enter heaven as a sinful human being. The good news is that Jesus took your punishment for sin and died on the cross in your place. "God commendeth [shows] His love toward us, in that, while we were yet sinners, Christ died for us" (Romans 5:8).

God also tells you to repent: "God … commandeth all men everywhere to repent" (Acts 17:30). Repentance is a change of mind that agrees with God that you are a sinner. Repentance also means you agree that Jesus died for your sins on the cross.

If you believe Jesus took your sins, died in your place, was buried, and then after three days rose from the dead, then you can truly call on the name of the Lord to be saved. Romans 10:14 promises us "whosoever shall call upon the name of the Lord shall be saved." God also recorded in His Holy Word that when the apostle Paul and his friend Silas were asked, "What must I do to be saved?" they replied, "Believe on the Lord Jesus Christ, and thou shalt be saved" (Acts 16:30–31).

If you have any doubts you are saved, or fear you would not be welcomed into heaven, you can pray right now to God, asking Him to save you. You can use this sample prayer:

Dear Jesus, I know I am a sinner. I believe, and I thank You for taking my sins on Yourself when You died on the cross. I believe You bled, died, and were buried, and three days later You were resurrected. All that You did so long ago was for me now. Please come into my heart and save me from hell. Thank You for Your forgiveness of my sins and Your gift of heaven and everlasting life.

If you prayed this prayer and sincerely and humbly meant it—you have called upon the name of the Lord Jesus Christ and believed on the Lord Jesus Christ— you are saved. You now have the assurance of going to heaven when you die. You made a very wise decision. The Bible tells us that "if thou shalt confess with thy mouth the Lord Jesus, and shalt believe in thine heart that God hath raised him from the dead, thou shalt be saved. For with the heart man believeth unto righteousness; and with the mouth confession is made unto salvation" (Romans 10:9–10).

This action cannot be undone. You are now a child of God, and His Holy Spirit is living within you. Do not be afraid to tell others about what you did. The same God who saved you is ready and willing to save your family and friends so they, too, can be assured of heaven.

Sincerely,

Mary Jane Humes

Acknowledgments

I am grateful for all of the people who helped me with this devotional.

My team of three editors:

1. My wonderful husband Joe, who faithfully and meticulously took my finished first draft, cleaned and tightened it up.

2. Then my favorite Uncle Ralph. We kept the post office busy with my manuscript going back and forth as he simultaneously critiqued, contemplated, and even complimented my work.

3. And finally Sally Hanan, my third set of eyes, who corrected any overlooked errors even while she put the finishing touches on this book.

Also, sincere thanks to Pastor Kevin Kline of Victory Bible Church, Paxinos, PA, who many years ago taught the Bible study on Genesis. It gave me a much fuller understanding and appreciation of Abraham. I am so grateful for the CDs of that to help me with the research for this devotional.

And always Christ Jesus, the most famous Son of Abraham, who gave His friend Abraham all those promises and made sure they were recorded in eternal holy writ. He not only keep His promises but also hears and answers our prayers today.

About the Author

Photo by Lindsey Hoke

Mary Jane Humes's desire to learn, coupled with a bit of adventure, led her into various job positions, a few of which actually utilized her BA in biology. Raised on a steady diet of books but no TV, she always had a dream of writing a book someday, so she started with *David's Faith* and *Abraham's Faith* is her fourth book. Currently she teaches Sunday school and plays the piano for her church.

When Mary Jane is not writing, she loves working on her property with her husband, Joseph, and caring for all of their rescued, furry little ones.

RESOURCES

Pick up your free prayer journal at:

https://maryjanehumes.com/free-prayer-journal/

CONTACT MARY JANE

LINKEDIN: linkedin.com/in/mary-jane-humes-72879b246
FACEBOOK: facebook.com/maryjanehumesauthor
EMAIL: hello@maryjanehumes.com
WEBSITE: maryjanehumes.com

Can You Help?

Reviews are everything to an author, because they mean a book is given more visibility. If you enjoyed this book, please review it on your favorite book review sites and tell your friends about it. Thank you!

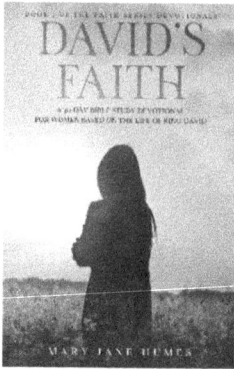

Imagine the story of King David coming alive (the boy who killed Goliath using only a stone, and a sling had many more exciting adventures) while you learn what God wants to teach you from these ancient histories to help you cope with your present life situations.

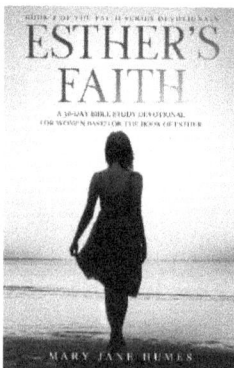

Learn from the woman who saved a nation. The story of Esther—orphan, woman of faith, intercessor, and queen can inspire us all to live out God's plan for our lives, and to leave legacies that will never be forgotten in *Esther's Faith*, an in-depth Bible study devotional of the book of Esther.

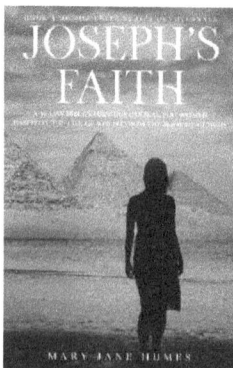

The encouraging and moving life journey of Joseph — goat herder, slave, household manager, prisoner, dream interpreter, and finally governor (highest official next to the pharaoh) — are recorded in the Biblical book of Genesis to help us learn how to trust God completely with His plans for our lives.

www.ingramcontent.com/pod-product-compliance
Lightning Source LLC
LaVergne TN
LVHW011350080426
835511LV00005B/224